Unshakable provi[des] storm. With each through His word, [worshi]p [a]n[d] [p]ray[er]. [W]e weren[']t designed to walk this life alone so invite your friends and small group to be part of an unshakable community!

~Kristianne Stewart
Founder/Compassion That Compels
CompassionThatCompels.org

This book is inspiring and encouraging. It is real and painfully honest. It is an amazing testimony of faith! Nancy doesn't just share her story, she offers Biblical examples and truth that will help and inspire you in your own storm. It's one I know I will read again and again. Read it yourself... and become unshakable.

~ Rosann Cunningham
Author, *UnEmployed Faith*
RosannCunningham.com

Anyone who argues the Bible isn't relevant for today needs to read *Unshakable!* Nancy shares openly about her struggle with fear and doubt. Thank you, Nancy, for sharing your story and for reminding us that God's promises are always true.

~Kristen Feola
Author, *Spiritually Strong* and *The Ultimate Guide to the Daniel Fast*
KristenFeola.com

Unshakable is an invaluable resource for those facing dark days. It strikes a beautiful balance between the struggle we face to fully put our trust in the Lord and the wholehearted faith we are challenged to have throughout Scripture.

~David Kennard
Pastor, Riverside Community Church, Oakmont, PA

It's refreshing when you come across a book that shares what it looks like to wrestle with God and yet still cling to Him as a fearful child clings to her daddy. *Unshakable* is not a book that brings God into our story; it beautifully displays how God brings us into His. I'm thankful that Nancy was willing to share her honest discoveries in her darkest hours.

~Heather Gilion
Co-author, *Dancing On My Ashes*
DancingOnMyAshes.com

Nancy demonstrates that it's possible to feel completely shaken by a difficult circumstance and yet come through it to find a faith that is unshakable...because of the God who is unshakable.

~Darcy Wiley
Blogger, www.MessageinaMasonJar.com

UNSHAKABLE:

Finding Faith to Weather the Storm

Nancy Backues

Copyright © 2015 by Nancy Backues

All rights reserved. This book or any portion thereof may not be reproduced or used in any manner whatsoever without the express written permission of the publisher except for the use of brief quotations in a book review.

Cover design by Crystal Brothers and Madi Walker
Cover photo © anibal / Dollar Photo Club

ISBN-13: 978-1511501774

ISBN-10: 1511501774

Unless otherwise indicated, Scripture quotations are taken from The Holy Bible, English Standard Version® (ESV®), copyright © 2001 by Crossway. Used by permission. All rights reserved.

THE HOLY BIBLE, NEW INTERNATIONAL VERSION®, NIV® Copyright © 1973, 1978, 1984, 2011 by Biblica, Inc.® Used by permission. All rights reserved worldwide.

Scripture quotations marked "The Message" are taken from *The Message*. Copyright © 1993, 1994, 1995, 1996, 2000, 2001, 2002. Used by permission of NavPress Publishing Group

DEDICATION

To my fellow warriors who have battled the demon of cancer

HOW TO GET THE MOST FROM THIS BOOK

This book was born from a labor of seeking answers, searching for hope, and finding truth. The foundation has been laid to pave the way for you to grow in your own faith. In each chapter you'll have a ringside seat for the physical, emotional, and spiritual battle against a powerful enemy: cancer. Your enemy may have another name, and your battle may look different, but the principles remain the same.

In the midst of each struggle, you'll journey back in time to visit characters from the Bible who faced equally hopeless situations. You'll learn from their struggles and be challenged by their faith.

Finally, you'll be given the opportunity to become *unshakable* in your own faith. At the end of each chapter is a section titled "Becoming Unshakable." In it, you will be challenged to read the text for yourself, answer a few questions, and complete a simple task to help you apply the truth in your everyday life.

God is certainly able to work in your life whether you complete the challenge or not. But if you are serious about developing faith that is *Unshakable*, it will require intentionality on your part. This book provides a place for you to start. Read the stories for yourself. Answer the questions honestly—either on the pages of this book or in your own private journal.

Before you know it, you'll find your faith becoming *Unshakable*.

CONTENTS

Foreword

Introduction

1. Shaken...1

2. Unshakable God: Is God Really Good 13

3. Unshakable Power: Is God Big Enough? 23

4. Unshakable Love: Does God Really Love Me? 33

5. Unshakable Purpose: God Has a Plan....................43

6. Unshakable Truth: God's Word is Truth................51

7. Unshakable Strength: God's Presence is Peace...........61

8. Unshakable Confidence: God Answers Prayer...........71

9. Unshakable Community: God Uses Others..............81

10. Unshakable Faith: God Isn't Finished Yet..............91

11. Unshakable Connection: God's Church...............102

12. Unshakable Victory: God Keeps His Promises.......112

Appendix: Becoming Part of God's Family................125

Notes...127

FOREWORD

There are moments when life seems to shift profoundly into something altogether unexpected and shakes the foundation of all you believe. In fact, that could be the very reason you hold this book in your hands. Perhaps you find yourself walking through an unwanted and difficult journey, and you're looking for something to stop the shaking of your soul.

Whatever circumstances have led you to these words, I am confident God is at work in your situation. He wants to speak to your heart and soul through the pages of this book.

In *Unshakable: Finding Faith to Weather the Storm*, Nancy shares her personal cancer journey with grace and honesty and opens up about the spiritual challenges and the victories she experienced along the way.

Her story and her faith will encourage you to look to heaven for strength and challenge you to face any stormy situation with confidence and courage. You will discover that God is with you; therefore, you can be *unshakable*.

Debbie Lindell
Lead Pastor/James River Church
Founder/Designed For Life Women's Conference

INTRODUCTION

In the summer of 2010, I noticed a strange lump in my hamstring. I shrugged it off, assuming it was the effect of the long road trip I'd recently taken and my newly rediscovered commitment to my treadmill. A few months later, I casually mentioned to my chiropractor that it was still bothering me. He examined the muscle and told me, "You need to see your primary doctor as soon as possible." I did, and she referred me to a surgeon. He wanted to do an MRI.

The results weren't good. I remember the exact spot in my kitchen where I stood listening to the voice mail from the surgeon: "You need to go to St. Louis immediately to see a specialist."

Until then, I had convinced myself it was nothing more than an especially stubborn muscle. Now there was no more denying the ugly truth: Something was wrong, and it was serious.

The "knot" turned out to be a 6-inch mass, and I was scheduled for surgery within two weeks. During surgery, doctors discovered the tumor was wrapped in a muscle and pressed against my sciatic nerve. They were able to remove the tumor but also had to remove the muscle in which it was tangled. They feared I would have permanent nerve damage, and possibly more serious damage, to my leg.

In the days following surgery, I focused on my recovery and tried to keep my mind on anything other than the pathology report we were waiting on. On my first post-op appointment, my worst fears were confirmed: the tumor was malignant. *I had cancer.*

The following weeks were filled with more scans, additional biopsies, discussion of treatment plans, endless "what-if" scenarios, and *a lot* of prayer. After the scans and biopsies were complete, doctors were satisfied the cancer had not spread. One month after my surgery, I was pronounced "cancer free."

Hearing the word "cancer" sets you on an immediate roller coaster emotionally. Although it was a short ride overall, it was made up of some of the longest moments of my life—moments of devastation, disappointment, discouragement, struggle, faith, commitment, determination, and then finally relief. Finally, the ride slowed and my world calmed with two simple words: cancer free.

Those words brought enormous relief, but my journey had not ended. We agreed to do radiation treatment to minimize the risk of recurrence. For two months following surgery, I had daily radiation treatments and bi-weekly physical therapy. At the end of those two months, I was ready to put it all behind me and move on with my life.

With a newfound appreciation for life and a determination to celebrate what God had done, I trained for, and completed, my first 5K—exactly one year after my surgery. I jumped back into life at full speed, and it wasn't long before cancer was a distant memory.

I lived cancer-free for three more years.

Then I unknowingly walked into the worst day of my life... a day that would leave me and my whole world shaken. I encountered something so devastating it shook me to the core and rattled everything I believed in.

This is my story—a story of shaken faith, and how it came to be *Unshakable*.

SHAKEN

*To what will you look for help if you
will not look to that which is
stronger than yourself?*

~C.S. Lewis [1]

I stepped out into the humid, August sunshine and breathed a sigh of relief. Another successful follow-up under my belt, I was free to go on about my life for another year. Then we'd do this all again.

We had the routine down: make arrangements for the kids, drive four hours, wait for a scan, wait for the doctor, have a brief conversation, and finally hear him say, "Everything looks good. We'll see you next year." Then we would make the four-hour drive back home and wait to do it again the following year. Yes, these appointments were necessary, but I was growing irritated at the need to do them at all.

I felt good. I had been cancer-free for three years now, and I was tired of experiencing the anxiety each "routine" visit created for me. Simply pulling up to the hospital created a whirlwind of butterflies in my gut. Walking the same halls I had been wheeled down for surgery three years earlier should have given me a sense of triumph. Instead, it filled me with dread. Every appointment brought a flood of thoughts and emotions, *What if they find something this time? What if my scan isn't clean? What if we have to do this all over again?* I was ready to put it all behind me. I wanted to be done.

Instead, I resolved to be content with my twelve months of freedom and left the hospital to meet up with my family. It was only a week until our kids started school, so we decided to make this trip a mini-vacation—a last hurrah of summer. I headed off to see the local sites with my husband and our eight- and five-year-old. Hours later we loaded our hot and weary bodies into the stifling heat of the minivan, eager to spend the rest of evening in the hotel pool. As we pulled out of the parking garage, my cell phone rang.

I recognized the number as the doctor's office, and my heart instinctively sank. We had been given the "all clear," and already scheduled an appointment for the following year. There was no reason for them to be calling me so soon...unless there was a problem.

I answered, reluctantly.

The young intern on the other end explained delicately: The radiologist had noticed "a suspicious spot" under my arm that had increased in size since the last scan...could I come back tomorrow for a biopsy?

That brief, three-minute phone call shattered my mood and ruined the rest of my evening. Unable to schedule my biopsy until the following Monday, I lived under a dark cloud of anxiety the entire weekend. I did my best to enjoy the rest of our vacation, but every activity—every moment—was overshadowed by worry and fear. I tried to rationalize away the anxiety, "It's probably a problem with the scan. Maybe they didn't read it right. I shouldn't worry until we know for sure what it is." My mind would be put at ease for about five minutes then wander back to the unknown. No matter how hard I tried, I couldn't come up with an explanation that would soothe my growing fear.

Monday found me at the hospital again. While I wanted to believe everything was fine, I sensed there was something terribly wrong. Although the medical staff was as warm and friendly as always, this visit felt very different from the others. I don't know if they could sense my anxiety or not, but they did their best to set me at ease. The doctor explained it was *highly unlikely* the cancer would spread to this location. Still, something in the tone of his voice caused my worry to grow.

I tried to distract myself by asking questions about the procedure and what to expect. But it was no use. I could feel my heart racing, my face growing warm, and my eyes growing watery. There was no stopping it. Soon, I felt big, hot tears rolling down my cheek. The staff did their best to calm me.

"It's just a biopsy."

"You won't feel a thing."

"It will all be over quickly, and you can go home."

They asked me about my family and where I was from, kindly trying to distract me, but nothing helped. I cried through the entire procedure. Since I had to lie perfectly still for the procedure, a sweet nurse wiped my tears with a tissue.

"Your eye shadow is so pretty," she said in a gentle, soothing tone. I was thankful for her kindness, but I couldn't help thinking, *I must really be a mess if she's complimenting me on my eye shadow!*

Once the procedure was over, I managed to pull myself together for the drive home. I knew what came next. It would be several days, maybe a week, before we would know the results. In the meantime, we would wait...and pray.

Family and friends who knew we had gone for a follow-up asked how it had gone. We tried to sound upbeat when we told them about the biopsy, but it was hard to mask the concern in our voices and hard to miss the worry in their responses.

We filled our days with the routine tasks that come with raising a family, trying to paint our world with a sense of normality. But in the rare moments when life quieted for a bit, fear and worry would raise their heads again. It was a constant struggle to keep our thoughts and emotions in check.

Finally, the call came: The biopsy was positive for soft tissue sarcoma...the same type of tumor that was removed from my leg three years earlier.

I managed to remain upright on the outside, but inside I crumbled. No one wants to hear, "It's cancer," but to someone who's been down that road before, those words carry extra weight—they undo all the fighting and bring immediate defeat. That simple statement stole every ounce of triumph—all the success of my previous battle—and left my emotions and my faith in a crumpled heap.

I had beat cancer once; I didn't want to have to do it again. To be honest, I wasn't sure I was up for the fight.

How many times did I have to fight this same battle?

How much could one person endure?

Where was God and why would He possibly allow this to happen?

I needed answers, but all I had were questions...*a lot* of questions. I couldn't help but think of the story of Job from the Bible. Although our circumstances were very different, I'm sure he experienced some of the same emotions I found myself facing.

More Than a Bad Day

Job is often heralded as the poster child of suffering, and rightly so. He endured more hardship than many of us can imagine.

He was a picture of success with a large, loving family (seven sons and three daughters), a successful business (*thousands* of head of livestock and a large number of employees), and a thriving personal life (he was "blameless" and "upright"). In fact, Job was the greatest man among his people (Job 1:3).

One day, Job received word that a group of traveling merchants had killed several of his servants and stolen his donkeys. As Job was listening to the account of the tragedy, another messenger arrived to inform him there had been a terrible fire, killing all his sheep and the servants tending them.

Job didn't even have time to process the news before yet another messenger arrived to say three raiding parties had invaded, stealing all the camels and killing even more of the servants.

Finally, one last message arrived: There had been a terrible tragedy. A mighty wind came and destroyed the house where Job's children were. They had all been killed.

In one afternoon, Job lost his business, his employees, his livelihood, and all of his children (Job 1:1-22).

But Job's trouble didn't end there.

A few days later, Job was stricken with painful sores from the top of his head to the soles of his feet. We don't know the official diagnosis of his condition, but we do know many of the symptoms: nightmares, scabs, disfigurement, weight loss, fever, and intense pain.

We often point to Job as the example of patience in suffering (and he is), but he didn't start out that way. He didn't immediately respond with unshakable faith in the midst of his storm. His initial response sounded very much like the way we respond when a storm shakes our life...Job threw up his hands in despair.

> *After this, Job opened his mouth and cursed the day of his birth. (Job 3:1)*

Job—the man who was "upright" and "blameless," the one who "feared God"—sat down and had a pity party. A well-deserved pity party, I'd say.

> *Oh that my vexation were weighed, and all my calamity laid in the balances! For then it would be heavier than the sand of the sea. (Job 6:2, 3)*

As a matter of fact, he grew quite vocal about his despair at times:

> *I will not restrain my mouth; I will speak in the anguish of my spirit; I will complain in the bitterness of my soul... (Job 7:11)*

Sometimes he got downright depressing:

I loathe my life; I would not live forever. Leave me alone, for my days are a breath... (Job 7:16)

For 37 chapters Job wallowed in despair. He would not be encouraged by his wife or his friends. He questioned God. He blamed God. He wondered if God had abandoned him.

God let Job speak his mind. He didn't interrupt Job in his sorrow. He didn't curse him for lack of faith. God let him get it all out. He let Job fully experience the roller coaster of emotions that come when the storm strikes: shock, fear, disappointment, despair.

I can relate to Job. I spent the weeks after my diagnosis wrestling with a range of overwhelming emotions. It took a long time for me to talk about it with anyone other than my husband and God. Even then, I rarely did so without crying.

Trusting God does not mean you deny or ignore your emotions. Trusting God means you don't camp out there.

God let Job experience his pain and despair, but He didn't let Job remain in it:

Then the LORD spoke to Job out of the whirlwind. (Job 38:1)

God responded to all of Job's questions and rants. For the next three chapters, God told Job, "Where were you when I spoke the worlds into existence? Oh, right...you weren't around, because you are *mortal*. And I am *God*. So, how 'bout you just trust Me and let me take care of this for you, OK?" (my paraphrase).

It would still take a few more chapters for Job to find his faith again, but when he did, he found comfort in God's response:

> *I know that you can do all things; no purpose of yours can be thwarted...I have uttered what I did not understand, things too wonderful for me to know, which I did not know.* (Job 42:2, 3)

Job didn't have to know *why* he was going "through the fire." He was content to know that God knew. He recognized that God was in control, and if God was in control, he was in good hands.

Faith is not the absence of emotion; it is the presence of Hope.

Like Job, there came a specific moment when God answered me out of my own whirlwind of emotions. He assured me He was right there, in the storm with me. So I had to decide: Was I going to wallow in my sorrow and let my emotions drag me under. Or, would I trust God and lean into His strength and stand on His hope?

> *We can't just sit around and wait for God to change our circumstances. We have to first rise on the inside, trusting that our God wants to deliver us.*
> ~Holly Wagner [2]

I determined that I would trust God. He had never failed me before, and I was sure He wouldn't start now. My life had been shaken—once again—by that ugly word "cancer," and I didn't have the strength to face it. But I know the One who is unshakable, and if I held tightly to Him, He would make me unshakable, too.

> *[God] only is my rock and my salvation, my fortress;*
> *I shall not be shaken. (Psalm 62:6)*

You may be shocked by the circumstances you find yourself in, but God isn't. You may be overwhelmed with the situation you are facing, but God's not. The test results, the pink slip, the divorce papers, the diagnosis...none of it caught Him off guard. He isn't wondering what He's going to do about it. He is still in control. And He wants to take your hand and lead you to the other side.

> *[God] knows the way that I take; when he has tried me,*
> *I shall come out as gold. (Job 23:10)*

Do you want to camp out in the midst of your pity party? Or would you rather take God's hand and see what He's going to do? I hope you chose the second option because that's where we're going in this book. We're going to learn how to grow in our faith, stake our claim on God's promises, and hold on to the One who is—forever—Unshakable.

Becoming Unshakable

In Job 3 we read of the devastation that left Job shaken. We feel his pain and anguish as he laments his situation and lashes out at God. However, by the end of the book, Job's perspective has changed (see chapters 38-42).

1. What circumstances have left you shaken?

2. How can you relate to Job's questions of God?

3. What other questions would you ask God?

4. Do you believe God sees your situation? Why or why not?

5. Do you believe God wants to bring you through your situation to victory?

Write out a prayer of desperation to God, either in your journal or in the space below. If you don't have a journal, consider starting one. Write out the situation that has left you shaken. Be honest about your emotions and how you feel about your circumstances. Don't worry; God is big enough to handle your brutal honesty. Ask God to show you how to navigate this storm, and commit to cling tightly to Him in the midst of it.

UNSHAKABLE

UNSHAKABLE GOD
Is God Really Good?

*Even in the middle of our pain,
perhaps more accurate, especially in the
middle of our pain, God is good.*
~Craig Groeschell[1]

Once we knew the cancer had returned, I immediately scheduled an appointment with my oncologist, desperately hoping he would have a reasonable explanation and tell me not to worry. He didn't. As a matter of fact, his usual pleasant demeanor had given way to serious concern. He ordered a thorough round of tests: more CT scans, a PET scan, even a brain MRI. I began the cycle all over again: scan, wait, and see the doctor for results. He would then schedule even more tests, and so on.

During those long days of waiting, life continued on around me.

The sun still rose. My kids still wanted breakfast and needed clean clothes to wear. Groceries needed to be purchased and floors needed to be swept.

To the outside observer I'm sure it seemed life continued as normal. But I stumbled through my days in a dense fog of questions, confusion, anxiety, and worry.

How far had the cancer spread?

Would I need another surgery?

What if I needed chemotherapy?

What does my future look like?

What does the future look like for my family?

It was August, and that meant the start of another school year. Of course, that meant school supply lists, teacher orientations, PTA meetings and all the other "normal" activities that come with launching children into a new phase of education.

That year should have been especially exciting as my youngest started Kindergarten. I had begun experiencing the familiar mix of excitement (I can get so much done!) and sadness (my baby is starting school!). But this new development—the dreaded "c" word—overshadowed any anticipation or excitement I felt for the coming school year. My baby was going to school, and all I could think about was what type and how many tumors were growing inside my body.

The night came to meet our children's teachers. Early that morning, I'd had another big, scary, worrisome scan, but that night I joined hundreds of other parents at school and pretended that the greatest worry I faced was finding the best price on glue sticks. We all stuffed our grown-up bodies into not-so-grown-up-sized desks, and I tried to absorb all the school-related information and fit it into the few nooks and crannies of my brain that weren't already consumed with medical jargon or anxiety.

I sat among the other parents of kindergarteners, recognizing the veterans—those who had older children and were familiar with school policies and routines. I also noticed the anxiety-ridden faces of those sending a child to school for the very first time. I watched the stress, the worry, the fear, and even the boredom on all their faces, and thought, *It's not fair, God. It's just not fair.*

Those parents were worried about buying the right notebooks or what type of snacks to send. They struggled to wrap their minds around pick-up and drop-off procedures. And here I sat in the midst of them worrying about tumors and trying to wrap my mind around treatment options.

It just wasn't fair.

I knew, at least on some level, that God isn't fair. He's just, yes. But fair? Thankfully, no, God is not fair. After all, if He was fair, we would all be doomed. God is perfect. He doesn't just *appear* to be perfect, He *is* perfect. He cannot tolerate imperfection, and believe me I've got plenty of imperfection! If God were *fair*, He would require that I pay for my imperfections (i.e., my sins). Romans 6:23 says the wages of sin is *death*. I'm glad that, instead of being fair, God is gracious and sent His Son to pay the penalty for my sin (Romans 5:8).

Still, I couldn't help but question God: *Why me? What had I done to deserve this? Why were other parents worried about school supply lists while I was worried about my future and my health?*

When God Doesn't Seem Fair...or Good

Job had every reason to question God, and he did just that.

> *Does it seem good to you to oppress, to despise the
> work of your hands? (Job 10:3)*

Job even questioned whether God was angry with him. He wondered if somehow his present circumstances were the making of a colossal prank for God's amusement. I'm sure Job wondered, as we all have at times, why God would allow such devastating circumstances to touch his life. After all, Job had done nothing but love and serve God. Still, he wondered if God was out to get him.

> *[God] has torn me in his wrath and hated me;
> he has gnashed his teeth at me. (Job 16:9).*

Job acknowledged God's sovereignty and His might but questioned His goodness.

> *His wisdom is profound, his power is vast. Who has resisted him and come out unscathed? He moves mountains without their knowing it and overturns them in his anger.... He performs wonders that cannot be fathomed, miracles that cannot be counted. (Job 9:4, 5, 10, NIV)*

Again, God let Job get it all off his chest before He finally had His say. When Job had finished his rant and, I'm sure, exhausted his emotions, God replied:

> *Who is this that darkens counsel by words without knowledge? Dress for action like a man; I will question you, and you make it known to me. (Job 38:2, 3)*

Basically, God told Job, "You have no idea what you're talking about."

Then He went on to ask Job a series of questions...

Where were you when I laid the earth's foundation?

Who set the earth on its axis and gave the seas their boundaries?

Who cues the sun to rise in the East and commands it to set in the West?

Who exists outside the confines of time and space?

Who can see darkness and light, the beginning and the end, life and death at the exact same time?

Where do I store the millions of snowflakes that fall in winter?

Where does lightning originate from?

Who commands the skies to let forth the rain?

Who tends to the animals, providing for their needs and granting them strength and instinct?

Who taught the eagle to build her nest and the hawk to soar among the clouds?

On and on God questioned Job, and Job got the message loud and clear: He was out of his league.

He had lashed out at God in his emotion. God did not deny him that privilege, but neither did He allow Job to remain in a state of hopelessness.

When your world is shaken, it's normal to question, or even blame, God. After all, if God really is good, how could He just stand by and let this terrible thing happen to you?

We cannot base our conclusion of God's goodness on the bad that happens in our world. While it may seem right at the time, the conclusion is irrational because it is based entirely on emotion. It fails to take into account the following:

We live in a fallen world. Adam and Eve walked away from God's plan and chose to disobey God's commands in the garden (Genesis 3). Their actions opened the door to sin as well as sickness, disease, and death. There *is* sickness in the world. There *is* disease. There *is* death. It is a result of man's disobedience to God and rejection of His original plan.

> *Just as sin came into the world through one man, and death through sin, and so death spread to all men because all sinned...* (Romans 5:12)

There are consequences to our actions. Some situations we find ourselves in are simply a result of poor choices on our part. If I choose to eat poorly and refuse to exercise for most of my life, there will be consequences related to my health and general well-being. If I choose to show up late, do poor work, and cause trouble at my job, I likely won't have that job for long. Not everything that happens to us is a result of our choices, but we do reap what we sow....in health, in relationships, in finances, and in life in general.

We cannot control the actions of others. If someone chooses to get behind the wheel of a vehicle while intoxicated, I cannot control the outcome of that situation or the effect it has on others. If someone chooses to detonate a bomb in a public venue, or open fire in a crowded building, I have little control over whether that choice affects me or others I know and love.

There is a spiritual battle waging around us. The Bible is clear there is a spiritual world—one we do not see but that greatly affects us.

We do not wrestle against flesh and blood, but against the rulers, against the authorities, against the cosmic powers over this present darkness, against the spiritual forces of evil in the heavenly places (Ephesians 6:12).

Sometimes the reason for our suffering is not related at all to our choices or the choices of others. There are times it is quite simply a spiritual struggle. There is no greater example of that than Job. (See Job 1 and 2.)

Can God intervene and heal sickness? Can He reverse the negative impact of our unwise choices? Can He supernaturally protect us from the crazed gunman or the natural disaster? Can He restrain the forces of evil and place us under supernatural protection?

He absolutely can, and often He does. So, why doesn't He do it every time? Quite honestly, I just don't know. My limited, finite mind rationalizes that if I were God, I would intervene every single time. But I am *not* God, so it seems rather egotistical of me to demand that the Creator of the universe explain himself to me.

Might the problem be less God's plan and more our limited perspective?

~Max Lucado[2]

If we cannot determine the goodness of God based on our circumstances and our emotional responses to them, how then can we know He really is good? As Christians we know one thing to be true...the Word of God. What does God's Word say about himself?

You are good and you do good. (Psalm 119:68)

When Moses asked to view God's glory, God's reply was, "I will cause my goodness to pass before you" (Exodus 33:19)...not His power or His might, but His goodness.

When Solomon prayed a dedication of the altar of God in the temple, he prayed that the people would "rejoice in [God's] goodness" (2 Chronicles 6:41).

The Psalmist staked his confidence in the goodness of God: "I remain confident of this: I will see the goodness of the LORD in the land of the living" (Psalm 27:13).

Peter reminds us that it is God's goodness that calls us to knowledge of himself (2 Peter 1:3).

We cannot base our belief of God's goodness on our current circumstances. If we do, we will only view our situation as hopeless. God is good...not because our lives are going well; He is good because *He is good.* When we settle in our hearts and minds that God is good, we can trust that He is working in our circumstances for our good.

Trust in the truth of God's Word...He *is* good. He *does* good. And He will do it for you.

Becoming Unshakable

In chapters 1 and 2 of the book of Job we discover what was really behind Job's situation: Satan himself had lashed a full-out attack on Job, his family, his character, and his faith.

1. Do you believe God is good? Why or why not?

2. What in your circumstances causes you to doubt God's goodness?

3. Can you relate to Job's questions of God in Job 10:3, 4? Why or why not?

4. Read the verses again about God's goodness on page 20. Explain what those verses mean to you.

5. How can you settle in your heart/mind that God is good and He desires to do good for you?

What other verses can you find on the goodness of God? Choose 3-5 verses to write out on notecards, and place them where you will see them every day (on your mirror, in your car, at your desk, etc.) When you begin to doubt God's goodness in your situation, turn to those verses.

3
UNSHAKABLE POWER
Is God Big Enough?

*When the ground beneath
my feet gives way,
and I hear the sound of crashing waves;
All my world is washing out to sea;
I'm hidden safe in the God
who never moves.*
~ Vertical Church Band[1]

The battery of scans my oncologist had ordered revealed both good and bad news. The cancer had not spread to my brain or to any major organs. That was the good news. But there was also bad news: there were a total of three tumors—the one under my arm that had already been biopsied, one in the muscle of my back, and a rather large mass in my abdomen. The cancer had not only returned; it had spread.

Since the biopsy had confirmed the one under my arm was the same type of cancer that was removed from my leg in 2010—a mixoid liposarcoma—it was assumed the others were, too.

Sarcomas make up less than 1% of all cancers, and there are 30 known types of sarcomas, making this particular type of cancer extremely rare. Historically, sarcomas have been treated with surgery...remove the tumor and hope/pray it doesn't return or spread. If it does return, it's typically treated with more surgery, so that's what my oncologist guessed would be the treatment. His partner agreed, so they sent me back to my surgeon.

Again, we made the four-hour drive to see the surgeon. He was confident the tumors could be removed. Since his specialty was orthopedics, he would do the one under my arm and in my back but would consult a colleague for the one in my abdomen. However, since sarcomas are very rare, he thought it would be a good idea to consult his colleague who was a sarcoma specialist. "See what he says, and if he wants to do surgery, we'll get you in."

Somehow, that set my mind at ease. I didn't necessarily want another surgery, but I had been down that road before. It wasn't easy, but it was doable. Surgery, a few weeks of recovery, and we would be done. Three doctors had suggested that would be the course of action, so I felt confident that would be the plan. We just needed this specialist—whom everyone seemed to think was *the guy* for this—to sign off on it.

The Specialist arrived with his entourage of medical personnel (because when one is *the specialist*, apparently people want to follow you around and learn how you do what you do). When the introductions and pleasantries were done, he cut straight to the chase. "The type of cancer you have is non-curative. We need to start chemo right away. Hopefully, we will be able to find something that works and keep it from spreading."

There it was...expressed as casually as if he was ordering lunch.

Wait. Did he say "non-curative?" As in, there is NO CURE?!

There were no statements like, "You're gonna beat this." "It looks very positive." Or, "We are hopeful." He simply blurted out those words, "non-curative," then launched into a barrage of information: recommendations of treatment, names of various chemo drugs and their potential side effects, treatment schedules, options for clinical trials, etc. The one thing he *didn't* mention was surgery.

"What about surgery?" I asked, unable to wrap my mind around the fact that three other oncologists had recommended surgery, and now it wasn't even an option.

"We could do surgery," he said reluctantly. "But I don't believe it's the best option."

He went on to explain they *could* remove the tumors, but they have not yet discovered how to keep *this* type of cancer from returning. If it returned or spread further after surgery, I would be too weak to do chemo. We needed to do chemo first and find the right drug that would control it (as sarcomas don't typically respond well to chemo).

"Surgery should *not* be the goal," he emphasized.

I struggled to reconcile this new information with the plan I had only recently accepted.

Then I asked the question no one should ever ask of an oncologist, "When you say 'non-curative,' that means…"

He simply stated: "You'll be on some type of chemo for the rest of your life."

Suddenly, time froze around me. The doctor continued to talk, but I couldn't hear anything he said as the news began to sink in. I sat in shock, my mind focused on his words: "chemo for the rest of your life." Although it would be months before we heard a doctor use these words, I had *stage 4 cancer.*

There had to be some mistake. I was a relatively healthy, 40-year-old, mother of two. Sure, I could stand to lose a few pounds, but my blood pressure, my cholesterol, all my numbers were good. In fact, I had just run two miles on my treadmill the night before. How could I have a disease considered *non-curative?!*

That meant *this* doctor...the one who was supposed to be THE GUY—the sarcoma *specialist*...didn't know how to get rid of *this* type of cancer. If *he* didn't know what to do, what hope did I have?

I left his office feeling overwhelmed and drowning in a sea of information I didn't understand. Somewhere between the hospital and the highway, God leaned in and whispered, "Do you think *I'm* big enough?"

In that moment, all the flannel board stories I heard as a child, all the late-night devotions, and every sermon I'd heard over the years started to pay off. Something "clicked" inside me, and I realized I'm not the first person to face circumstances that seemed impossible. The Bible is full of such examples. In fact many of them had *no* hope of making it out alive.

Into the Fire

If you managed to stay awake in your World History class, you might recall the name Nebuchadnezzar; he was the king of Babylon. When Nebuchadnezzar conquered Jerusalem, he took the best and the brightest young Hebrew men captive. Among those men were Daniel, Shadrach, Meshach, and Abednego (Daniel 3).

Nebuchadnezzar was also quite the ego-maniac and soon decided to erect a 90-foot statue of himself. As if a giant statue wasn't enough, he planned a great celebration so everyone could come and worship his statue. As devoted followers of the One True God, Shadrach, Meshach, and Abednego refused to worship Nebuchadnezzar's idol. As you can imagine, Nebuchadnezzar didn't care for their resistance. He made a law stating that anyone who refused to worship the idol would be thrown into a blazing furnace.

Word spread of the Hebrew boys' defiance, and Nebuchadnezzar had the boys brought to him. Graciously, he gave them one more chance, explaining the consequences they would face if they refused. Maybe they had simply misunderstood the instructions.

Instead of obeying the king's command, the boys replied:

If we are thrown into the blazing furnace, the God we serve is able to deliver us from it, and he will deliver us from Your Majesty's hand. (Daniel 3:17, NIV).

The God we serve is able...*He is BIG ENOUGH.*

Their response infuriated King Nebuchadnezzar, and he ordered the furnace be heated seven times hotter. The heat was so intense, it overcame and killed the men who were ordered to bind the boys and throw them into the fire!

Now, if I were God, that's where I would have created the escape route...guards are overcome and killed, boys escape, everyone lives happily ever after.

But that's not what happened. The Hebrew boys fell into the fire—the already-lethal-then-heated-seven-times-hotter fire, the fire that had overcome and killed the guards who were *close* to the fire. Now the Hebrew boys were *in* the fire. Their situation went from bad to really bad to *impossible*. There was no getting out of this one. There was no hope.

27

You could say their situation was hopeless, that the fire was "non-curative."

When King Nebuchadnezzar went to check on the fire, he didn't find the dead bodies of the three Hebrew boys. Instead, he found them up and walking around...*in* the fire! And there were one...two...three...FOUR of them!

God never lets you walk through the fire alone. He's always right there with you.

The king had the boys brought out of the fire and cleaned off. Not only did they survive the fire, their clothes weren't even burnt; in fact, they didn't even smell like smoke!

When you walk through fire you shall not be burned, and the flame shall not consume you. For I am the Lord your God... (Isaiah 43:3)

God was big enough to deliver them *from* the fire, but instead He chose to deliver them *through* the fire. Why? Well, I'm not God so I can't know for sure, but if I had to guess, I'd say it's because of what happened next...

Nebuchadnezzar answered and said, "Blessed be the God of Shadrach, Meshach, and Abednego, who has sent his angel and delivered his servants, who trusted in him...for there is no other god who is able to rescue in this way." (Daniel 3:28, 29)

God had a greater plan. His plan included more than simply getting three Hebrew boys out of a pinch. His plan included turning the heart of a king.

God is bigger than a 90-foot statue. He's bigger than a narcissistic tyrant. He's bigger than a blazing fire. And in that moment, as we left the specialist, He reminded me that He is bigger than cancer.

If I had to face cancer and chemotherapy in my own strength, you'd find me in the fetal position over in the corner. If I had to "beat this" with my own ability, I would be hopeless. If my *only* hope was in my doctors and their knowledge of cancer (as vast as it is) I would be defeated. But to the One who spoke light into existence and knit together every cell of my body, cancer is no big thing.

As we drove home from the doctor's office with the seemingly hopeless news that this cancer was "non-curative," I realized the God I pray to for healing is the same God who created our universe out of nothing. (Genesis 1)

He's the One who blew back the waters so an entire nation could cross the Red Sea on dry land. (Exodus 14)

He's the One who helped a young boy with a few rocks defeat a seasoned soldier. (1 Samuel 17)

He's the One who healed a woman of a 12-year medical battle with a single touch. (Mark 5)

He's the One who called Lazarus from the grave when he'd already been dead four days. (John 11)

And He's the One who walked out of the tomb after three days, defeating sin, sickness, and death. (Matthew 28)

These are more than stories to spark the imagination of children in Sunday school. They are actual, historical events. Moments when God stepped into the everyday moments of ordinary people…and miracles happened.

This God—He is THE ONE for my situation.

> *God is infinitely bigger than your biggest problem.*
> ~Mark Batterson [2]

While I was shocked at the diagnosis, God was not.

While doctors are baffled by this rare form of cancer, God is not. He is the Author of all life. If He can reverse a chronic medical condition and call a dead man from the grave, He can correct a few cells in my body that have gone haywire.

This same God knows your situation, too. He sees whatever you face today. He is not shocked by it. He is not scared or intimidated by it. He is (more than) big enough.

> *God can do anything, you know—far more than you could ever imagine or guess or request in your wildest dreams!*
> (Ephesians 3:20, The Message)

Becoming Unshakable

Shadrach, Meshach, and Abednego took an amazing step of faith. They defied their boss—a narcissistic tyrant—and said, "We are throwing ourselves into the hands of our God." They could not have known at the time what far-reaching effects their faith would have. Read the full story in Daniel 3:1-30.

1. Why do you think Shadrach, Meshach, and Abednego were able to remain so confident in their faith?

2. What things (situations, emotions, etc.) tend to shake your confidence in God?

3. Do you believe God is big enough to handle what you are facing? Why or why not?

4. What can you do to overcome those doubts? List some things that will help you trust God's ability to work in your situation.

5. What can you do when you begin to feel discouraged?

Find and read your favorite Bible story. Imagine yourself as the character in the midst of that story, without knowing the outcome. How would you feel? As you pray for your current situation, remind yourself that God sees your situation, He already knows the outcome, and He's walking through it with you.

UNSHAKABLE LOVE
Does God Really Love Me?

*It is not what God can do,
but what we know He yearns to do,
that inspires faith.*
~F.F. Bosworth [1]

We left the specialist's office with the words "non-curative" and "chemotherapy right away" still hanging in the air. Our minds and emotions reeled. My husband and I had a three-hour drive to pick up our kids, then another three hours home, but we needed to process what we'd just learned. Although neither of us had an appetite, we decided to stop at a restaurant and put together the few pieces of information we were both able to retain.

After what seemed like hours of staring at our food, praying together, and crying together, we resolved to do whatever needed to be done and trust God for the rest.

We knew the next step was to determine what to say to others. So far, we had only told a few family members and close friends what was going on. We had asked them to pray for our appointment, and they would be waiting to hear what we learned. We had to start making phone calls on the long drive home, and I knew the first call had to be to my parents.

How do you have that conversation? How do tell the people who still worry that you won't have enough gas to make it home (even though you're a 40-year-old woman with a family of her own) that the specialist doesn't know what to do? How do you call the people who sat up every weekend in your teens to make sure you made it home safely and tell them you're scared you might die and leave your children behind?

How do you tell your siblings and your in-laws that everything is *not* fine as it has been every other time you've talked? How do you bring up the fact that you're about to start the battle of your life...*for* your life?

How do you spring it on your friends over lunch that you'll be starting chemotherapy soon? Or mention it casually to other parents in the neighborhood because there might be questions when you have to shave your head?

I don't know that there's an easy way. I think you just do it.

And that's exactly what I did.

I picked up the phone and called my parents. They had been praying for our appointment and were waiting for an update. They put the phone on speaker so they could both hear.

I tried to keep my voice calm; I didn't want to give them any reason to worry. And I did *not* want to cry; I might not ever stop.

I explained what the doctor had said: there are three tumors. They are non-curative, which means some sort of chemotherapy for the rest of my life.

They don't know how to keep it from coming back again and again and again.

We hadn't determined a specific treatment plan yet, but he had given us some options.

We had a lot to consider and to pray about.

After all the logistical questions had been answered and I felt myself reaching the end of my *everything-is-OK-don't-worry* voice, my dad asked one final question:

"OK, Nanc…what do you need?"

I wanted to crumple into a heap of tears and crawl into my Daddy's lap like the scared little girl I was. I wanted him to kiss my forehead and promise me it would be all right; he would take care of everything. I wanted him to soothe my worries and my fears the way he used to when my biggest fear was what lurked inside my dark closet. And I'm sure he wanted the same thing. I know, if he could, my dad would move heaven and Earth to keep me from this battle.

The Love of a Father

Sometimes as Christians we have no trouble viewing Jesus as our Brother or Advocate, on our side and in our corner. But we have a hard time seeing God as our Father. Angry judge? Sure. Righteous and vindictive? Possibly. Aloof and uncaring? Potentially. But loving Father? Doubtful.

These preconceived ideas of God seem to be confirmed when we face a tragic or hopeless situation. "See!" we say, "God is out to get me!" Or, "Where is God now? I knew He didn't care!"

It's one thing to sit in Sunday school as a child and belt out "Jesus Loves Me" with heartfelt enthusiasm. It's another thing altogether to face a job loss, a ruined relationship, or a cancer diagnosis as an adult and say with conviction, "Yes, my Father loves me."

We can accept the fact that God loves the world *in general* (as in John 3:16), but how can we be sure He really loves me, individually...you, individually...your mom, your sister, your neighbor, individually. Even if we believe He *knows* our situation and *can move* in our situation, how can we know for sure He cares enough to do so?

The Lord longs to be gracious to you; therefore he will rise up to show you compassion. (Isaiah 30:18, NIV)

The Father of compassion and the God of all comfort, who comforts us in all our troubles... (2 Corinthians 1:3, NIV)

Once again, we need to see past the emotion of our situation and turn to what we know is true: We have to look at how God describes His relationship with us in His Word:

Creator: *"Then God said, 'Let us make man in our image, after our likeness.'" (Genesis 1:26).* We were God's idea, and we are His creation. He didn't speak us into existence only to twirl us out into space and let us fend for ourselves. His relationship with us didn't end once He breathed life into Adam. When Adam blew it in the garden, God pursued him (Genesis 3:8, 9). When Israel turned on God again...and again...and again, God pursued them (Isaiah 44:21, 22). And when we fail God...again...and again...and again, He doesn't give up on us. We were created *for* Him...to have a relationship *with* Him.

Shepherd: *"I am the good shepherd. The good shepherd lays down his life for the sheep."* *(John 10:11)* We don't understand much about shepherding in the modern, Western culture, but it's a concept that would have been familiar to the people in both Old and New Testaments. They would have understood the heart of the shepherd toward his sheep. They would have known that a shepherd would go to great lengths to provide for and protect his sheep, even sacrificing his own life to ensure their protection. By referring to himself as the good shepherd, Christ was saying that He will go to great lengths to provide for and protect *His* sheep (i.e., you and me!)

Savior: *"But God demonstrates his own love for us in this: While we were still sinners, Christ died for us"* *(Romans 5:8)*. Perhaps the most compelling argument for God's love for us is the fact that when we had nothing to offer Him...when all of our best intentions and greatest accomplishments only add up to rubbish (Isaiah 64:6), God still loved us. He showed us His love by sending His Son to die in our place (the penalty of sin), so that He could have a relationship with us...which was His original plan all along.

Father: *"Those who are led by the Spirit of God are the children of God."* *(Romans 8:14)*. Now that I'm a parent, I understand more clearly parental love. Sometimes one of my children will claim he or she feels "no one loves them"—not because he or she is abused or mistreated but simply because they are being corrected or trained in discipline at that moment. Does my love for them change in that moment? No. They *feel* unloved because of an emotional response to their circumstances. But my love for them never changes, just as God's love for us never changes.

We cannot build our belief of God's love on our present emotions, just as we cannot build our belief of God's goodness on our present situation. Sometimes we can be like children, *feeling* unloved by God because our circumstances have grown difficult. But God's love for us is unwavering…it is unshakable. Our circumstances may change. Our emotions *will* change. But God's love for us will *never* change.

I am blessed to have a very loving earthly father, so it's not difficult for me to see God as a loving Heavenly Father. I know my earthly father would do everything in his power to take care of me. Why would my Heavenly Father do anything less?

> *If you then, who are evil, know how to give good gifts to your children, how much more will your Father who is in heaven give good things to those who ask him! (Matthew 7:9, 10)*

I realize not everyone has (or had) a loving relationship with his or her earthly father. If that is true for you, I am deeply sorry; please know God is not like your earthly father. He is not waiting for you to fail. He is not mad at you. He is not disappointed in you. He will not abandon you. He loves you, and He wants to show you just how great His love is for you. You can't do anything to make God love you any more, or any less, than He already does. He already loves you perfectly.

> *There is no pit so deep that God's love is not deeper still.*
>
> ~Corrie ten Boom [2]

We were created to have relationship with God. He loves us and pursues us, even when we fail. All we have to do is realize how much we need Him and accept His gift of love. It's truly that simple.

> *This is how God showed his love for us: God sent his only Son into the world so we might live through him. This is the kind of love we are talking about—not that we once upon a time loved God, but that he loved us and sent his Son as a sacrifice to clear away our sins and the damage they've done to our relationship with God. (1 John 4:9, 10 The Message)*

When we acknowledge our need for God and accept His love through salvation, He adopts us into His family and calls us His children.

> *But to all who did receive him, who believed in his name, he gave the right to become children of God. (John 1:12)*

If you have accepted Christ as Savior, then God *is* your Father. He loves you. He wants the best for you. Don't let your emotional response to your situation convince you otherwise.

> *See what great love the Father has lavished on us, that we should be called children of God! (1 John 3:1)*

Could it be that God didn't abandon you in your situation? Could it be that He is waiting with great, big, wide-open Daddy arms for you to come running to Him so He can make it all right again?

Becoming Unshakable

In John 10:1-42 Jesus compared himself to a shepherd. Read the passage to see how He described His relationship with us and explained His relationship to God the Father.

1. How would you describe your relationship with your earthly father?

2. What words would you use to describe God?

3. Read the following passages. How does each passage describe God? Genesis 1 & 2, John 1:12, Romans 8:5, 1 John 4:8

4. How has your relationship with your earthly father influenced your view of God?

5. Write a letter to God describing your earthly father. Tell God what you loved about him and the ways he disappointed you. Then read the letter again. Consider how God is like your father and how He is unlike your earthly father.

Have you accepted Christ as Savior? Is He Lord of your life? If you would answer "no," then you are at odds with Him (James 4:4). God still loves you. In fact, He doesn't want to be at odds with anyone. He wants everyone to be a part of His family, and He made a way for that to happen by sending His Son, Jesus, to die as payment for our sins. If you'd like to know more about a relationship with God, see Becoming Part of God's Family on page 125.

UNSHAKABLE

UNSHAKABLE PURPOSE
God Has a Plan

*If You wanna steal my show,
I'll sit back and watch You go;
If You've got something to say,
go on and take it away...*
~Toby Mac[1]

Before my diagnosis I had big plans. With my youngest starting Kindergarten, I would finally have some time to myself to do things I wanted to do: I could find time for a regular work-out routine or volunteer at church or my kids' school. I might even get around to cleaning out that basement closet I'd avoided for the last three years!

I heard other moms lament, "I don't know what I'm going to do with myself when my baby goes to school!" I couldn't relate; I had notebooks full of ideas!

One thing I had *not* planned for was cancer, but that's exactly what happened. It not only inserted itself on my to-do list, it consumed my time, emotions, and mental energy, leaving little time for *anything* else.

When I first got the diagnosis, I was shocked. Then I was devastated. Then I was *ticked off*.

Didn't God know what I had planned?! Hadn't He seen the lists and the notebooks full of ideas?! I was pretty sure I had run the ideas by Him. Volunteer...*at church*. Offer my time and talents...to my kids' school. These were *good* things!

One afternoon, in the midst of my pity party/rant, a friend sent me a text with this verse: The Lord says, "I will guide you along the best pathway for your life. I will advise you and watch over you." (Psalm 32:8, NLT)

That stopped me mid-rant. What could that possibly mean?!

It was not your typical "I'm praying for you, you're gonna make it" verse I had received from so many others. You know, verses saying "Do not fear..." "I am with You..." "Nothing is impossible with God..." Those verses left me feeling encouraged, uplifted, warm and fuzzy. But...

I will guide you along the best path for your life?!

How could cancer possibly be the best path for my life?

As I thought about it, I wondered, *Could it be that God had another plan...one that was less about* me *and* my *agenda and more about* Him *and* His *plan?*

Check, Check, Check

As a self-proclaimed, Type-A planner: I like my lists. I like my plans. I like sticking to my plans. And I *love* accomplishing things because then I can cross them off my list! There's a woman in the Bible to whom I can relate; her name was Martha. I have a feeling Martha loved her lists, too, because when Jesus came to her house, she busied herself *doing* things (Luke 10:38-42). A woman after my own heart!

Martha, her sister Mary, and their brother Lazarus were friends of Jesus. Their lives experienced a storm when Lazarus became very sick (John 11:1). Martha and Mary sent word to Jesus that Lazarus was not well. Like any good Type-A multi-tasker, I'm sure Martha thought she was simply being efficient. After all, Jesus happened to also be the Messiah, so two birds, one stone: inform Jesus of Lazarus's illness, solicit healing from the Healer himself. Check and check.

When Jesus received the message, he kept right on doing what he was doing…for another *two days*. I can only imagine the frenzy this sent Martha into. She probably passed the time by puttering around the house, tending to Lazarus, snapping at poor Mary, and all the while muttering under her breath about what could possibly be taking Jesus so long!

Then Lazarus died. That was *not* what Martha had planned, I'm sure. She had done everything right, sending word to Jesus of Lazarus's illness. I'm sure she assumed Jesus would rush right over and make Lazarus well again. But He didn't.

When Jesus *finally* came, Lazarus had been dead for four days! Always on top of things, Martha met Jesus outside of town:

> *Martha said to Jesus, "Lord, if you had been here, my brother would not have died. But even now I know that whatever you ask from God, God will give you." (John 11:21, 22)*

If I were Martha, this is what that would have meant: "Lord, it's about time You got here. Let's not waste any more time. Lazarus is dead. Just say the word and You can be on your way. Then we can get on with our lives."

What Martha did not realize was Jesus already had a plan. When He had received word of Lazarus's sickness, He already knew the outcome:

> *This illness does not lead to death. It is for the glory of God, so that the Son of God may be glorified through it. (John 11:4)*

Nowhere, on any of Martha's lists, did it read "Lazarus dies to glorify God." If it had been up to Martha, it would have gone something like this: Lazarus gets sick, send word to Jesus, Jesus speaks healing, Lazarus recovers. Check, check, check, and check. Done.

God had a different plan. He didn't worry. He didn't fret. He didn't need to rush or hurry. It was *His* plan, and it was unshakable.

When Jesus arrived at Lazarus' house, He was not shaken by the news of Lazarus's death. He was not shaken by Martha's worry or anxiety. He knew the plan.

He went to the tomb and prayed to God. Then He called out to Lazarus. The corpse of a man who had been dead for four days drew breath again. Lazarus stood up and walked out of the tomb! This happened in front of hundreds of people: friends, family members, and professional mourners.

God's plan...check.

This is God's Word on the subject: "I know what I'm doing. I have it all planned out—plans to take care of you, not abandon you, plans to give you the future you hope for.
(Jeremiah 29:11, The Message)

Let me be clear: God *did not* give me cancer. But He knew I had cancer long before I did. He did not cause it, but He did allow it...for a time. And if He allowed it, He must have a plan in it. That's how He works.

God knew what he was doing from the very beginning. He decided from the outset to shape the lives of those who love him along the same lines as the life of his Son.
(Romans 8:28, The Message)

God is eternal, which means He exists beyond the confines of time. He sees *all* of time at the same time. He sees the end as well as the beginning. That's how Jesus could calmly, and confidently say, "This sickness will not end in death" when He received word about Lazarus.

However, knowing the plan does not mean God is unfeeling or uncompassionate to your circumstances. Jesus knew Lazarus would be raised from the dead, but that did not keep Him from feeling the emotion of the situation and weeping for his friends (John 11:35).

God loves us so much that He hurts when we hurt. Even when He sees the end—even when He knows the outcome will be good—He feels the pain of our circumstances.

God sees your situation. No matter how shocking it was to you, it did not catch Him off guard. He is not worried about it. Nor is He uncompassionate toward it.

> *God is powerful enough to change your situation and personal enough to enter into the emotion of it.*
> ~John Lindell[2]

It may feel like your circumstances are beyond your control; there may be a lot of things about your situation you *can't* control. But one thing you *can* control is your response to it.

I had not planned on cancer or chemotherapy, but I still faced it. I had to decide whether I would allow God to use it for good. Or would I wallow in self-pity and grow bitter over the fact that He allowed it at all?

If I believe that God is good, He loves me, and He is in control, then it makes sense for me to let go of my plans. Instead of writing *my* agenda, it makes sense to hand over my list and let God write His story. I have a feeling His will be much better than mine would have been anyway!

Becoming Unshakable

John 11:1-45 details one of the greatest miracles of Jesus' ministry—the raising of Lazarus from the dead. But it's also one of the most personal stories in the Gospels. In this story, we not only witness the miracle, we also see how deeply it affected Jesus on a personal level.

1. What plans did you have that have been wrecked by your circumstances?

2. Whom do you most relate to in this story?

3. Have you ever felt like God's answer to your prayer was delayed? How did you handle that delay?

4. Whose plan do you trust more, yours or God's? Why?

5. What potential ways do you see that God can be glorified by your situation?

In your journal, list some ways your plans have been sidelined by your current situation. Then pray and give each one to God. Commit to setting aside your agenda and ask God to help you rest in His plan.

UNSHAKABLE TRUTH
God's Word is True

*When you understand what God's Word
says about the battle you face,
it changes your countenance.*
~*Priscilla Shirer*[1]

Time slowed to a crawl as I stumbled through my days in a fog, my head swimming with medical terms and my mind racing with potential scenarios. It had only been a few short weeks since the initial biopsy that rocked my world, but it seemed like years. At times, it was difficult to focus on anything other than the fact that I had cancer.

We had left the specialist's office with a sea of information, a stack of papers to read, and a list of treatment options to consider. Since his office was four hours from home, we decided to explore options in our hometown—that meant additional doctors, more appointments, and even more scans.

As I waited for my name to be called early one morning in yet *another* waiting room, I could feel the weight of the last few weeks settling in on me. I was nervous and cold despite the attempts of the friendly nurse to calm me and the thin blanket to warm me. I'd had many scans over the last three years, but this one was different. This time I knew what they would find; I knew I had cancer. There was no coming out of this with good news.

When they called my name, I explained to the nurse that my veins tend to roll, making it difficult to draw blood and typically requiring several attempts. (After three years of routine blood draws, you learn to lead with that type of information.) She smiled kindly and assured me she was used to it. She prepped my arm, then gave me a warning: "Quick poke!" and stuck the needle into my arm. True to form, my vein dodged the needle and left the vial empty.

The nurse apologized and tried again. I had grown accustomed to hospital personnel needing multiple attempts to draw blood, but I wasn't up to it that day. I felt my eyes began to water. Then big, wet tears spilled out down my cheeks.

I tried to stop them. I tried to hold them in, but it was no use. They had started and they wouldn't stop. The nurse finally found a vein and quickly drew the blood she needed. The pain stopped, but the tears kept coming.

I was led to a patient waiting area…and I continued to cry. They called me back to the radiology room…and I still cried. It was as if all the worry, all the fear, all the things I tried not to feel since the initial biopsy came flooding to the surface with the prick of that needle.

The poor technician taking my medical history didn't know what to do with this blubbering mess before him. He asked me the questions as quickly as he could, gently handed me some tissues then excused himself and left the room. A few minutes later, a kind, grandfatherly fellow came in. He sat down across from me, leaned forward and gently asked, "Are you OK?"

I shook my head and continued to sob.

He looked at my chart and said, "You've had this before, right?"

I nodded...and sobbed some more.

He gently explained that the scan would be painless and that I was doing the right thing. He assured me I was in good hands; his people were the best. He stayed and talked with me for several minutes.

He didn't tell me anything I didn't already know, but I still began to feel better. I don't know if it was his gentle voice, his quiet confidence, or the fact that he was a cancer survivor himself. Something in our conversation soothed my emotions and calmed my nerves. After a few minutes, he gave me a warm blanket and left me to "relax" in the quiet room while I waited for my scan.

That's when I remembered my phone...and my Bible app. I dug the phone out of my purse, put in my ear buds, and drifted off to sleep as God's Word soothed my soul.

When it was time for my scan, the technician returned and led me to another room with a large machine and a small, thin table. As I lay on the table and the machine began to whir, I felt the familiar fear creeping back in. My thoughts, and my heart, began to race. My mind was on the fast track to hysteria again—but this time I got control.

I searched my memory desperately to recall verses people had sent me in texts and e-mails:

When I am afraid, I put my trust in you. In God I trust and am not afraid. (Psalm 56:3, 4)

> *Fear not, for I am with you; be not dismayed, for I am your God; I will strengthen you, I will help you, I will uphold you with my righteous right hand. (Isaiah 41:10)*

> *It is the Lord who goes before you. He will be with you; he will not leave you or forsake you. Do not fear or be dismayed. (Deuteronomy 31:8)*

I spent the next 45 minutes quoting every verse I could remember from Sunday School, Scripture calendars, lessons I had written and taught, and my own Bible study. I sang every Scripture song I could think of and when my memory failed, I quoted verses loosely in my own paraphrase.

> *Worry is the sin of distrusting the promises and the power of God. It's choosing to dwell on the worst-case scenario. It's faith in the bad things rather than faith in God.*
> ~Craig Groeschel[2]

As I began to meditate on God's Word, my thoughts slowly turned from my own worry and anxiety to God and His goodness. My heartbeat slowed, and my body relaxed. My mind filled with peace—so much peace, in fact, that I dozed off a few more times during the scan!

When we're in the midst of the storm, our thoughts tend to run away and take our emotions with them. If we're not careful, they can take us to a very dark and lonely place, and it can happen very quickly.

We become consumed with thoughts like:

How can this be happening?

Why me?

What am I going to do now?

I don't know if I can get through this.

What does this mean for my family?

What does my future look like?

As I struggled to wrap my mind around the cancer diagnosis, and all that it meant, I quickly realized that while it was important to be informed of the diagnosis and explore my options, it did me no good to worry about the future.

> *Whatever is true, whatever is noble, whatever is right, whatever is pure, whatever is lovely, whatever is admirable—if anything is excellent or praiseworthy—think about such things...And the God of peace will be with you.*
> *(Philippian 4:8)*

I had to balance my intake of overwhelming, often discouraging, information with what I know to be true and right...the Word of God. When I began to focus on the Word of God, I began to experience God's peace.

It is Written

Even Jesus used God's Word against the attacks of fear and doubt.

> *After fasting forty days and forty nights, [Jesus] was hungry.*
> *(Matthew 4:2)*

I love the simplicity of this statement. Jesus had not eaten in *forty days*, and the Bible simply says He was hungry. I don't know about you, but after a few hours without food, I am famished! The point is Jesus was weak. Yes, even as the Son of God, He felt hunger and weakness in His human flesh...just as we do.

Satan took the opportunity when Jesus was feeling weak and run down to mess with His thoughts and emotions. The enemy's tactics haven't changed much over the years: It's when we're the weakest and the weariest that the enemy sees an opportunity to pounce.

> *Your adversary the devil prowls around like a roaring lion, seeking someone to devour.* (1 Peter 5:8)

I've often wondered why Jesus didn't flex His supernatural muscles at this point in the story and show Satan a thing or two. He could have called down a band of warrior ninja-angels (you know they were waiting for His signal). He could have flicked Satan in the forehead or just said, "Scat!" and the devil would have scampered away like a frightened alley cat.

Instead, He made a very simple statement: "It is written..."

Could it be that He wanted to give us an example? That He wanted us to know when it comes to combatting the lies of the enemy (like fear, anxiety, and worry), it's not about how big your spiritual muscles are; it's simply about standing on the Word of God?

Three times Satan came at Jesus in different scenarios and with different temptations.

Three times, Jesus replied with the same statement: "It is written…"

After the third time, Satan had nothing left. He had no option but to give up and retreat (Matthew 4:11). Jesus-3, Satan-0.

I believe this story is included in the Bible to teach us a very profound and practical lesson: There is power in the Word of God.

There is power to calm fears.

There is power to settle anxiety.

There is power to overcome worry.

There is power to defeat the enemy.

But in order to *use* the power in the Word of God, we have to *know* the Word of God. This is where Jesus had a definite advantage over us. Since He wrote it, He's infinitely more familiar with it than we are. Still, the principle remains: There is power in the Word of God, and when we use the Word of God, we access its power.

Here's the trick: We can't *know* the Word unless we *read* it. Profound, I know.

It seems like such a simple concept: You have to read it to know it. But so many times, that's where we miss it. It's hard enough to find time to regularly read God's Word in the busyness of normal life. The additional stress of a medical diagnosis, a failed relationship, a job loss, or other form of life-storm will definitely sideline your devotional time until you eventually find yourself consumed entirely with your circumstances instead of God's Word—unless you are intentional about it.

Here are three simple ways to do just that:

Read Scripture. I'd like to say my Bible reading was consistent *before* I faced cancer, but in reality, the demands of day-to-day life often crowded it out. Suddenly, I was desperate, and I needed to hear from God. Reading my Bible became a priority once again. I chose a time and a place and made a commitment to it—every day. If something unexpected derailed my appointed time, I made a point to keep my commitment at another time that day.

If you don't know where to start, read through Psalms. The Psalmist faced some serious, life-threatening circumstances. The Psalms are full of beautiful examples of people finding strength to weather the storms of life.

Write Scripture. As I came across passages I knew I would need to remember, I printed them out (or just wrote them on notepaper) and taped them to my mirror, my refrigerator, in my car...anywhere I knew I would see it *daily* to remind myself of God's Word and His promises.

Memorize Scripture. I've never been so thankful for all those memory verses I learned in Sunday school and at youth camp. If you didn't grow up in church, it's not too late to start memorizing Scripture. Find a verse that means a lot to you and repeat it to yourself over and over until you remember it. I have quoted entire sections of Psalms while sitting in doctor offices or having scans. Nothing calms the nerves like the promises of God!

You keep him in perfect peace whose mind is stayed on you, because he trusts in you. (Isaiah 26:3)

Becoming Unshakable

Even Jesus battled fatigue, temptation, and attacks from the enemy. If the Son of God was not immune to the mental games the enemy plays, neither are we! Read Matthew 4:1-11 to see what Jesus did when He faced the attacks of the enemy.

1. How has your situation affected your thought life?

2. What messages do you allow your mind to "feed" on (media, music, books, etc.)?

3. What Scripture passages have meant the most to you through the years?

4. How would you describe your personal devotional time? How much time do you spend reading God's Word?

5. What are some practical things you can do to control your thoughts of worry, anxiety, and fear?

Commit to spending time in God's Word every day this week. It may be 5, 15, 30 minutes, or longer. The length of time doesn't matter as much as the consistency. Determine a time and place and keep that appointment. Find a verse you want to memorize; write it out and post it where you can see it every day. Work hard to memorize that verse (or verses) this week.

UNSHAKABLE STRENGTH
God's Presence is Peace

*Praise the Lord with the world
on your shoulders;
Praise the Lord when it seems too hard;
Praise the Lord 'cause in
every moment Jesus Christ is Lord.*

~ *The City Harmonic*[1]

After exploring our options, we had decided to do my treatment locally. Not only would it save us the eight-hour round trip each week, but we wouldn't have to try to juggle child care, work schedules, and the other hundreds of details that need to be worked out when parents need to travel hundreds of miles on a weekly basis.

We discovered that I could receive the same treatment at our local cancer center that I would have at the specialist's office. By staying close to home, there would be less disruption to our day-to-day routine, especially for our children. My husband would be available to take our kids to school and pick them up. Plus, it would be easier for him to rearrange his work schedule for a few hours each week and either return to work or work from home.

The specialist and the local oncologist would work together to coordinate and monitor my treatment. The specialist would oversee the "big picture" from four hours away while the local doctor would handle the day-to-day details of my treatment, side effects, and weekly bloodwork. Both assured me they did this often and had even worked together many times before. It seemed like a flawless plan and somehow made things a little less overwhelming.

We scheduled an appointment with the local oncologist, assuming we would set up a schedule and finally begin the process. However, that was not the case.

Not only was he reluctant to schedule treatment right away, he questioned the specialist's recommendation for chemotherapy. Admitting sarcomas were not his area of expertise, he agreed to confer with our specialist directly and assured us he'd be in touch.

A complicated medical diagnosis often means many *different* doctors will be involved. And when many doctors are involved, you can be sure many *differing* opinions will be, too.

We left the office and walked to our vehicle in stunned silence. It had taken so much energy and emotional strength to get to this point…to come to grips with the fact that chemo was the best option at this point rather than surgery, to wade through the barrage of information about treatment options and facilities, then to finally reach a decision and schedule the appointment. Now we were going home again with more questions instead of answers. We were only a few weeks into the journey, and we were already overwhelmed, frustrated, and exhausted.

All I wanted to do was cry, even though that was about *all* I had done for the past few weeks.

My emotions were overloaded, and I didn't know how much more I could take. I was sure I couldn't hold it together any longer.

My husband returned to work, and I had two hours to myself before our kids came home from school. There was plenty to be done—laundry, dishes, dinner prep, a number of other tasks routinely performed by the Home Manager. But I didn't care much about what needed to be done. I was focused on what *I* needed to do, and I knew exactly what that was.

I went home, turned on worship music, and buried my face in the couch. I couldn't find words to even pray. I just cried and sang.

Then I cried some more.

Suddenly, I realized the words I was singing...

You hear me when I call
You are my morning song
Though darkness fills the night
It cannot hide the Light
Whom Shall I Fear...

My emotions began to turn...from despair to determination.

From fear to hope...

I know who goes before me
I know who stands behind
The God of Angel Armies
Is always by my side

The one who reigns forever
He is a friend of mine

> *The God of Angel Armies*
> *Is always by my side*
>
> *My strength is in Your Name*
> *For You alone can save*
> *You will deliver me*
> *Yours is the victory*
> *Whom shall I fear*
> *Whom Shall I Fear*

By the time I made it to the bridge, my tears had dissolved into peace, and dare I say...confidence?

> *Nothing formed against me shall stand*
> *You hold the whole world in your hand*
> *I'm holding on to your promises*
> *You are faithful*
> *You are faithful?*

When the storm hits and our world is shaken, it's not our natural instinct to raise our hands and worship. Cry? Yes. Murmur and complain? Absolutely. Rant about the injustice? Definitely. But sing praises to God? Definitely not.

Unlikely Praise

If anyone deserved to rant about his circumstances, it was the Apostle Paul as he sat in a Roman prison. Paul and his colleague, Silas, had been going around doing good...preaching the Gospel, praying for people, and delivering servant girls from demon oppression (Acts 16:16-18). It was actually that last one that got them into so much trouble.

When the girl's owners/employers heard that their servant girl had been freed, bringing their lucrative, fortune-telling business to a screeching halt, they had Paul and Silas hauled into court. The two men were stripped and publicly beaten with rods. Then they were thrown into a Roman prison and their feet bound in stocks (Acts 16:19-24).

> *About midnight Paul and Silas were praying and singing hymns to God, and the other prisoners were listening to them. (Acts 16:25)*

It's just one small verse in the whole story, and if you're not careful you can blaze right past it: Paul and Silas were praying and *singing hymns to God!*

They had just been beaten within an inch of their lives then thrown into prison *unjustly*. All they had done was help a poor servant girl who was being used and abused. For that, they were beaten and imprisoned.

I understand the praying…I would be doing that, too. God and I would be having a serious conversation, but singing?! Maybe *after* God had answered my prayer and released me. Perhaps I'd feel like worshiping *after* He had poured out vengeance on those who treated me unfairly. Maybe *after* God had come through for me. Yes, then—definitely then—I would feel like having a worship service. I might even break out the tambourines and streamers.

But Paul didn't wait for the answer. He understood some principles we often forget in the midst of our trials:

Worship is not about us and our circumstances; worship is about God and Who He is. Our circumstances may change. Our emotions *will* change. But God will *never* change.

He is the same yesterday, today, and forever. That means He is just as worthy of our worship at midnight in the middle of a Roman prison as He is when the day breaks and we reach the mountaintop.

Ascribe to the Lord the glory due his name; worship the Lord in the splendor of his holiness (Psalm 29:2).

Worship redirects our emotions. It takes the focus off me and what I can do and puts it on God and what He can do.

Our circumstances might seem overwhelming, and maybe they *are* overwhelming when we look at them with our limited perspective. But when we worship God, we realize we are not limited to our own strength, wisdom, or resources.

Worship reminds us that we are connected to ultimate strength, unlimited wisdom, and unfathomable resources. How then can we remain overwhelmed, anxious, and fearful? We simply can't.

How can we *not* be strengthened when we are listening to, and singing, messages like…

> *Your name is higher; Your name is greater*
> *All my hope is in You.*
> *Your word unfailing; Your promise unchanging*
> *All my hope is in You*[3]

> *Lord, I need You, oh, I need You, Every hour I need You*
> *My one defense, my righteousness*
> *Oh God, how I need You*[4]

> *Your grace abounds in deepest waters,*
> *Your sovereign hand will be my guide,*
> *Where feet may fail and fear surrounds me,*
> *You've never failed, and You won't start now*[5]

Those words, and the messages they convey, can't help but take root in our hearts, in our minds, and in our spirits. It's impossible to remain hopeless and in a state of despair while you're proclaiming how great God is!

> *The place of praise is not just after God moves. It is an entry point into the presence of God and the moving of His power.*
> *~Brian Houston* [2]

Worship makes the way for a miracle. Something amazing happened when Paul and Silas began to worship God: the prison doors flew open and their chains fell off. They worshiped first *then* they saw God move on their behalf.

Does God sometimes move without our worship? Sure. But sometimes He moves *in response* to it. Paul and Silas didn't wait until God had delivered them from prison before they began to praise Him. And we shouldn't wait until God delivers us before we worship Him.

> *You are my hiding place. You protect me from trouble. You surround me with songs of victory. (Psalm 32:7, NLT)*

Becoming Unshakable

It's so much easier to sing God's praises when things are going well in our lives, but it's so much more *necessary* to praise God in the midst of the storm. Read how Paul and Silas did just that in Acts 16:16-34.

1. How would you define "worship"?

2. What obstacles in your life keep you from worshiping God?

3. Is your worship of God based on your emotional response to your circumstances or the fact that God is worthy of our worship? Explain.

4. How does worship redirect your emotions?

5. What are some of your favorite worship songs/albums?

Set aside a specific time each day this week to worship God. Turn on some of your favorite worship music. Write out your worship to God in your journal. Play, sing, or write a song of thanks to God. Go for a walk and thank God for everything you see along the way. Spend time consciously thanking God for Who He is and what He's done for you.

UNSHAKABLE

UNSHAKABLE CONFIDENCE
God Answers Prayer

Miracles are the by-product of prayers that were prayed by you or for you...that should be all the motivation you need to pray.
~Mark Batterson [1]

When you hear the word "cancer," it feels like a death sentence. When you sit across from a specialist and he looks you squarely in the eye and tells you the cancer is "non-curative," you wonder if it really is a death sentence. It shakes you...*to your core.*

Even when you come to grips with the truth that God is good and He is working for *your* good. Even once you understand how much God loves you and how He *longs* to do good for you. Even when you've tamed your thoughts and wrestled your emotions by standing on God's Word and singing His praises. There comes a time when another doctor looks at you and says *again*, "We can't cure the cancer; we can only try to control it." Sometimes, in that moment, you are strong, and you stand boldly in your faith. Sometimes, you crumple. Up is down. Black is white. And everything is gray.

In those moments, I knew I had to cling to something—Someone—stronger than myself. I had to hold onto Someone unshakable. If doctors didn't know what to do, and *I* certainly didn't know what to do, I had to appeal to a Higher Power.

I know God moves in response to prayer, and I believe the Bible when it says the prayer of a righteous man (or woman) is powerful and effective (James 5:16). I remember often as a child watching my dad on his knees, face buried in the seat of a chair, crying out to God for whatever we (or a loved one) needed at the time.

It's not just a *theory* I adhere to or a Sunday school lesson I've been taught. It's a practice I've seen in action. I haven't just read it in the Bible or in stories of missionaries in far-off lands. I've experienced it in my own life and the lives of my family members.

I had seen God answer prayer for provision, wisdom, guidance, and miraculous healing. I had experienced many of these answers to prayer in my own life and the lives of my family. For years, I prayed for others with great determination, believing that prayer moves the hand of God. If there was ever time to put that belief to the test, *this* was that time. I needed God to show up. I needed Him to move in my situation. I needed Him to intervene for me, for my health, and for my family.

There was one problem. I didn't *feel* like praying. I wasn't sure I could; I didn't even know what to say. But I *knew* I needed to pray, so I did.

At first, my prayers were simple: "God, help me. I need you."

There was no fanfare, and to be honest, very little faith, just a simple, heartfelt cry of desperation. I had been praying my whole life, but suddenly I didn't have the words to say or the faith to back them up.

> *The prayers of godly people recorded in Scripture are examples of straightforward honesty. When they were afraid, they told God about their fears. When they doubted, they doubted out loud in front of God. When they were angry, they let it rip.*
> ~Craig Groeschell[2]

I needed to enlist others...people who could carry me in prayer until I could stand on my own faith again. We gathered our small group from church. These were families with whom we had walked through very difficult times together. We had also shared incredible victories with each other. They were a group with whom we did life—the good, the bad, and the ugly. This was definitely ugly. We needed them, and we knew they would be there for us. We shared our fears, our worries, and our commitment to trust God in the process. They gathered around us, laid hands on my husband and me, and prayed. *And our faith grew a little.*

I emailed a few women whom I know have great faith; they immediately began to pray. *And my faith grew a little more.*

We were added to prayer lists at churches of friends and coworkers. Teachers at our kids' school stopped me in the halls and told me they were praying for me and for our family. *And our faith grew a little more.*

We rearranged our volunteer schedule at church so we could be in the service each week when they had prayer for the sick. We went forward for prayer every single week. We committed to attend the weekly prayer service on Wednesday evenings. *And our faith grew a little more.*

As others prayed *for* me, a strange thing happened. My faith grew, and I began to find the words to pray on my own again. Not only did I pray because I *needed* to, I began to pray because I *wanted* to. I blocked off sections of time in my day to spend in prayer. *And my faith grew a little more.*

In those moments God began to speak to me. There was never an earth-shaking voice from heaven. I never heard trumpets sound or angels sing. Sometimes it was a gentle "nudge" in my spirit. Other times, it was just a sweet, calm, peace. But God showed up…every time.

> *In every situation, by prayer and petition, with thanksgiving, present your requests to God. And the peace of God, which transcends all understanding, will guard your hearts and your minds in Christ Jesus. (Philippians 4:6, 7 NIV)*

Often we think of prayer as something we have to be "qualified" to do. We believe we need special credentials to come before God and make audacious requests for things like healing. After all, God is Sovereign, and if He wants to heal, then He can certainly do so without us pestering Him. But that's not what the Bible says about it:

> *Is anyone among you sick? Let him call for the elders of the church, and let them pray over him, anointing him with oil in the name of the Lord. And the prayer of faith will save the one who is sick, and the Lord will raise him up. (James 5:14, 15)*

God wants us to pray. If you are suffering, the Bible says to pray. You don't need any special degrees. God doesn't require certain letters behind your name to call on Him. He uses everyday folks just like you, and me, and a man in the Bible named Elijah.

Rain's a Comin'

Elijah was a man with a nature like ours, and he prayed fervently that it might not rain, and for three years and six months it did not rain on the earth. Then he prayed again, and heaven gave rain, and the earth bore its fruit.
(James 5:17, 18)

The nation of Israel, God's chosen people, had turned their backs on God. They had forgotten all He had done for them by delivering them from Egypt and bringing them to the Promised Land. Rather than following God, they had allowed their rebellious king, Ahab, to lead them down a dark path of idolatry. Instead of worshiping the One True God, they began to worship Baal, the god of fertility and lord of the rain clouds[3].

But there was one man, Elijah, who loved God and remained faithful to Him. Elijah prayed there would be no rain. And there wasn't...for more than three years!

Things had become so severe that the king grew furious with Elijah, forcing Elijah to go into hiding. Even while he was hiding from an evil king, God was looking out for Elijah, providing water from a brook and food delivered by ravens (1 Kings 17:4). After three years, God told Elijah to return to Ahab and tell him it will rain again.

After many days the word of the Lord came to Elijah, in the third year, saying, "Go, show yourself to Ahab, and I will send rain upon the earth." (1 Kings 18:1)

Elijah went to Ahab and challenged the false prophets of Baal to a battle of the gods. Despite their best efforts, the prophets of Baal were no match for God, and in the end they were utterly humiliated (1 Kings 18:17-40). After a smashing victory over the false prophets, Elijah told the king to feast and celebrate because after three years of severe drought, rain was coming. Then Elijah climbed to the top of Mt. Carmel to pray (1 Kings 18:42).

Elijah prayed. God had already promised He would send the rain, but Elijah still prayed. Elijah recognized that prayer wasn't about convincing God to do something...God had already promised He would. Prayer is about our obedience and submission to Him.

Elijah *kept praying*. He didn't toss a little prayer out into the wind and go on his way. He prayed, and when he didn't see the answer. He prayed again. Still, no rain...not even a cloud. Seven times he prayed, and looked, and prayed again, and looked again.

He said to his servant, "Go up now, look toward the sea." And he went up and looked and said, "There is nothing." And he said, "Go again," seven times. (1 Kings 18:43)

Finally, the seventh time his servant said, "There's a teeny, tiny cloud waaaaaay off in the distance."

At the seventh time he said, "Behold, a little cloud like a man's hand is rising from the sea." (1 Kings 18:44)

Elijah didn't give up because he understood when we are faithful to pray, God is faithful to work in our lives and in our circumstances.

Elijah believed. Immediately he told his servant to rush to Ahab, before the rain stopped him.

Go up, say to Ahab, "Prepare your chariot and go down, lest the rain stop you." (1 Kings 18:44b)

That is faith, my friend. After three years of drought, a tiny cloud appeared on the horizon, and Elijah immediately trusted that God had kept His promise. He had sent rain. Before the first drop fell, before the cloud appeared, Elijah took God at His Word.

And in a little while the heavens grew black with clouds and wind, and there was a great rain. (1 Kings 18:45)

When your world has been shaken, the greatest thing you can do is pray. It doesn't have to be long. It doesn't have to be eloquent. It doesn't even have to be coherent. Sometimes, in those darkest moments, our heart-cries are all it takes. God understands. He hears our hearts when our words fail.

As we pray, our perspective begins to shift. The problems that once seemed so large—so overwhelming—begin to seem so manageable. As we come before an Almighty God and lay our problems at His feet, as we pray Scripture and remind ourselves of His promises, and as we experience His presence and remember how good He truly is, we find that our faith is strengthened and we can rise again to the challenge, because He has promised to be with us.

And when we look to the skies, and we still don't see rain...when the sun is beating down just as heavily as it was before—when the doctor's report is discouraging, when the divorce papers come, when the company goes under—we come back to our knees and pray again.

Because when we say we believe in the power of prayer, it's more than a line we learned in Sunday school. When we say, "God hears the prayers of His people," they're not just words we read in an inspirational book. When we're in need of our own miracle, and we fall to our knees believing He is listening, God leans in to whisper, "Yes, I still do miracles. And I can do one for you."

The eyes of the LORD are toward the righteous and his ears toward their cry. (Psalm 34:15)

Becoming Unshakable

Unless we keep our eyes focused on God and our minds set on His promises, it is difficult to see Him working in our circumstances. But when we put our trust in God, and take Him at His word, we can have confidence that He will do what He has promised to do. We can have the same confidence that Elijah had. Read the full story in 1 Kings 18:1-46.

1. How would you describe your belief in the power of prayer?

2. What prayers has God answered for you in the past?

3. When should someone *stop* praying for something?

4. What do you do when you don't feel like praying?

5. How can you find faith when it feels like your prayers are not being heard or answered?

Be bold in your requests to God this week. Ask Him to work a miracle in your situation. Write out your requests in your journal (or in the space below). Be sure to make note of when your prayers are answered, too. If you find your faith is struggling, write out the verses in this chapter to remind yourself of God's promises.

UNSHAKABLE COMMUNITY
Don't Do It Alone

*It's not the load that breaks you down,
it's the way you carry it.*

~Lena Horne [1]

    I awoke early on Monday, September 9, 2013. Honestly, I hadn't slept much through the night. It was my birthday, but it wasn't excitement that kept me from sleep. It was anxiety. Today was the day I would start chemotherapy.

    After much consultation, the oncologist and the specialist had decided chemo would be the best course of action. And after much prayer, we decided to trust them. So on the morning of my 41st birthday I would report to the hospital for a minor outpatient surgery to have a port (a small, implanted device used for delivering chemotherapy drugs to your body) placed under my skin. Then I would drive across the street to the cancer center for my first round of chemotherapy.

    Happy birthday to me.

It's one thing to come to grips with the fact that you will have chemotherapy "soon"; it's another thing entirely to wake up knowing that today is the day—the day you officially become a cancer patient. I knew God was in control. I believed we were doing the right thing. I had faith that God would walk with me through this.

I had wrestled with my emotions and my faith. I had resolved in my mind and my heart that God is good, He loves me, and He is big enough for my situation. I had grounded myself in His Word and in worship. I had prayed, and prayed, and prayed some more. I had struggled and won against the fear and anxiety. I had looked people in the eye and said with confidence, "God is with me; we'll get through this."

There had been moments—not many, but some—when I would wonder in the back of my mind, "Will I really get through this?" There were moments when fear would creep in, and I would worry about my husband and my children: How would they weather this storm? There were occasional, brief moments of doubt when I would think, "Did I really hear from God? Does He *really* see what I'm going through?"

In those moments, I would do what I knew to do. I would fight the battle again. I would go to God's Word. I would get on my knees. I would lift my hands and my voice in worship until I had once again quieted the voice of fear. I would gather my courage and my strength and steady myself for the fight, because you have to fight a lot of battles before you win the war.

But today I was tired. I didn't want to fight. I didn't want to get out of bed and go to chemo. I wanted to crawl under the covers and hide. I had fought the spiritual and emotional battles, and I was worn out. Now I was faced with reality....surgery and chemo. I didn't want to do it, and I wasn't sure I had any strength left to make myself.

I reached for my phone to check the time and noticed a text message. *That's odd,* I thought. I knew the name well, but it was odd that she would text me overnight...at 2:00 a.m., to be exact. For a brief moment, curiosity overrode my fear...what could be so urgent at 2:00 a.m.?

This is what it said:

> Hi, Nancy. I know you're sleeping but the Lord woke me up to pray for you, so I just wanted you to know you are being lifted up! He is in control and He's not afraid of the future because our God knows the plans He has for you—He can't wait to show you how he's going to use you thru this trial to advance His kingdom. Your family is safe because He's holding them, too! He's not surprised by any of this and He will be by your side the whole way. I can't wait for us to see the good things that come from this hard thing. The Lord is your strength! Chemo's got nothing on the Creator of the universe! He has already given you the grace you need to get thru this. Don't be scared!!! God is going before you to every doctor visit, every chemo round, every question, and every conversation that is to come. You are strong because Christ has made you that way so tonight I'm praying for courage and boldness in the coming weeks, for strength from the Father, for rest, for peace, and for the presence of God to surround you and your home. You're not alone. And you are loved.

As I read those words, tears began to flow. Each line was like balm to my battle-weary soul, soothing my wounds and calming my fears.

I had just seen this friend the night before when I had felt strong and confident. She was aware of what I was facing the following day, but we hadn't really discussed it. I doubt she could have known the fears that lingered deep inside me. I'm not sure I had even known.

But God knew.

And He woke a young girl, someone a generation younger than me, and allowed her to be an answer to my unuttered prayer. She could have sent a simple, "Praying for you" or a timely verse, and it would have been greatly appreciated. But God used her to send me a very specific message: *I see you. I know your fears. Don't worry; I have everything under control.*

Not only had God heard my prayers for faith, for help, and for healing, He had heard the unprayed cries of my heart for practical and emotional support. Before I even realized what practical needs we faced, God laid it on the hearts of others to be "Jesus with skin on." Time and again, friends and family unknowingly became timely "love notes" from God, reminding my husband and me that He knew *exactly* what we were facing and what we needed.

When I struggled with thoughts of fear and doubt, I would often receive a text asking how I was doing. There's no way the sender could have known what I felt at that moment, but God knew. And when I allowed myself to reply honestly about the struggle I felt, God used the other person to strengthen my faith and leave me encouraged.

When I was desperate for God's Word, but had no idea where to start, friends sent Scriptures recounting promises of God's faithfulness and healing. When I faced another doctor appointment, and potentially discouraging news, friends and family members e-mailed to say they were praying for me…on that day, at that time.

When we decided to do chemotherapy, my friends threw me a party to celebrate the fact that I was not alone in this battle. They bought me beautiful hats, scarves, jewelry, and chocolate…lots of chocolate! Family members offered to come and help us during my treatment. My mom, my sister, and my mother-in-law took turns coming to care for the house, keep up with the laundry, cook meals, and manage the kids and their schedules with minimal interruption. Friends drove me to appointments and sat with me during treatment.

When my hair fell out in huge clumps, a friend showed up on my doorstep—clippers and drape in hand—to shave my head in the privacy of my own home. When I ventured into public with my bald head wrapped in a scarf for the first time, friends met me with smiles, hugs, and words of love and encouragement.

When I couldn't read any more about the disease and its treatments, friends took me out for coffee and a good laugh.

Carry each other's burdens, and in this way you will fulfill the law of Christ. (Galatians 6:2, NIV)

To say we were blessed is an understatement. God surrounded us with people who met our needs, carried our burdens, and encouraged our spirits. When you have family and friends who are willing to go into battle with you, you truly feel you can do anything…just ask Jonathan.

An Army of Two

Jonathan was the son of Saul, king of Israel. Not only was he the king's son, he was a pretty decent soldier in his own right. As Israel faced their arch-enemy, the Philistines, they found themselves at a disadvantage.

The Philistines had a larger army and had claimed the higher ground. Their camp sat at the top of a ravine while Israel was camped in the valley (1 Samuel 14:4, 5). Suddenly, Jonathan got a crazy idea. What if he climbed up to the Philistine camp and took them by surprise? Maybe, just maybe, God would give him victory. Jonathan told only one person about his plan...not his father the king, not his fellow soldiers, only his armor-bearer.

We don't even know the man's name, but we do know that as an armor-bearer, he would have been selected for his bravery and dedication. Not only would he have carried Jonathan's armor for him, he would have committed to stand by him in times of danger[2].

Jonathan confided his outrageous plan to his armor-bearer: They would show themselves to the enemy. If the Philistines said, "We're coming down to you," Jonathan and the armor-bearer would fight with all their strength. If the Philistines replied, "Come on up!" that would be the sign that God would give the two Israelite soldiers victory. They would climb the steep cliff and defeat the Philistines.

I'm not a military strategist, but that seems like an unlikely scenario to me. That didn't deter Jonathan's armor-bearer, however. I love his response:

"Do all that you have in mind," his armor-bearer said. "Go ahead; I am with you heart and soul." (1 Samuel 14:7)

Basically, the armor-bearer said, "Let's do it, Jonathan. I'm all in."

I don't know why he responded that way when the odds were clearly stacked against him, but I love that he did. Maybe he had an unnatural thirst for adventure. Maybe he was an adrenaline junkie. Or, maybe he realized that no one should go into battle alone.

He committed to stick with Jonathan through thick and thin, "heart and soul." So Jonathan and his dedicated armor-bearer came out of hiding right into plain sight of their enemy. Seeing a golden opportunity, the Philistines said, "Come on up, we'll teach you a thing or two!" (They weren't dummies!) So Jonathan climbed the cliff with his armor-bearer close behind. They reached the top and...

> *The Philistines fell before Jonathan, and his armor-bearer followed and killed behind him. In that first attack Jonathan and his armor-bearer killed some twenty men in an area of about half an acre. (1 Samuel 14:13, 14)*

They killed twenty men! Not only did they beat all tactical odds and deliver a crushing blow to the enemy, their little field trip struck fear into the hearts of the entire Philistine army!

> *Then panic struck the whole army—those in the camp and field, and those in the outposts and raiding parties— and the ground shook. It was a panic sent by God. (1 Samuel 14:15)*

God never intended us to do life alone, and He certainly doesn't want us to do battle alone.

When you're in the midst of the storm, there are moments you can't stand on your own two feet. You need people who will stand for you and hold you up. You need people of faith who will be your "faith legs" until you can stand on your own again. You need people of strength to carry you when you're battle-weary and can't go on. You need people who will say, "Do what you need to do...I am with you, heart and soul."

When the storm hits, it's not time to be independent and isolated. It's time to lean on those around you who are willing (and wanting) to help any way they can. Accept offers of meals, child care, house cleaning, prayer, encouragement, and any other need that can be met by someone else. You may even need to swallow your pride and *ask* for help if necessary.

> *Two are better than one, because they have a good return for their labor: If either of them falls down, one can help the other up. But pity anyone who falls and has no one to help them up (Ecclesiastes 4:9, 10)*

After offering to bring a meal for my family, one friend followed her offer with this statement: "Please don't rob me of my blessing." Those words struck me. I'd never thought of it that way. I knew *I* enjoyed helping others when they were in need, but I never thought of it the other way around. *They* were being blessed by helping *me* in my need. Who was I to stand in the way of that?

Becoming Unshakable

God calls us to go into battle together...whether it's our battle or our friend's. Jonathan's armor-bearer thought nothing of joining Jonathan. It wasn't his battle, but he fought alongside his friend because of his commitment to him. Read the full story in 1 Samuel 14:1-15.

1. What is the nicest thing someone has done for you?

2. Who is the one person you rely on when you're at your weakest?

3. What needs do you have that can be met by others while you are facing this trial?

4. Who can you ask for help with those needs?

5. How are you able to help others in their need?

Make a list of things you know you need done (meals cooked, home cleaned, errands run, transportation, child care, etc.) Look at the list and determine what can be done by others. When someone asks what you need, refer to the list and take them up on the offer!

UNSHAKABLE FAITH
God Isn't Finished Yet

When all we know is doubt and fear;
There is only One Foundation,
We believe, we believe.
~Newsboys [1]

After four months of weekly visits to my oncologist's office, you'd think I'd have grown used to it, but I hadn't. Each time I pulled off the highway and saw the towering building with the words "Cancer Center," the same old, familiar feelings washed over me—dread, fear, anxiety.

The pit in my stomach would grow as I pulled into the parking lot and walked through the front doors. By the time I made it to the waiting room on the sixth floor, my heart would be pounding and my pulse racing.

It didn't matter that I passed the building countless times in my regular routine without experiencing any of those emotions. It didn't matter that I had completed six rounds of chemo, and the PET scans showed the cancer was responding well. It didn't seem to matter that the tumors had shrunk to almost half their original size. It didn't even matter that the specialist was genuinely surprised by the success of the treatment—so surprised, in fact, that he had told me I no longer needed to see him unless the tumors grew again.

None of that mattered now. What mattered was that I had completed the prescribed treatments and the cancer was still there.

Thanks to the practical, emotional, and spiritual support of our family and friends we had made it through the fall and even enjoyed the holidays with relatively minimal disruption from the treatments. But now we were in the New Year. It was January, and I had no idea what this year held for me or for my family.

Like everyone else, I had done my fair share of reflection and planning in the last few days. I thought back to the previous January when I had cancer and didn't even know it. I reflected on the events of the previous year—the birthdays and other family events we had celebrated, not knowing what lay ahead of us. Then the dreaded moment at the end of the summer when our lives, our schedules, and our faith had been shaken.

I was thankful God had been there in that moment and had continued to walk with us through each moment since. He had given us wisdom in wading through information and options. He had strengthened our faith and given us indescribable peace. He had surrounded us with a support system that was beyond anything we could have hoped for. He even gave me grace to weather the treatments with minimal impact on my body and to our routines.

So, what did this new year hold in store for us? Would we face even greater obstacles than we had the previous year?

Would we look back and be awestruck at how far God had brought us?

As we waited for the doctor, I couldn't help but think—hope—that *this* would be the moment I got my miracle. *This* would be the time the doctor would come in and say in amazement, "I don't know what happened, but we can't see any cancer. It's gone!" And I would whoop and holler and shout and give God all the glory. Maybe *this* was that time.

Perhaps God had waited until the chemo was done to grant me a miracle so there would be no question that it was God. Of course, that must be it.

The doctor came in, and I nervously squeezed my husband's hand, my spirit swelling with faith.

"Well," the doctor said hesitantly, "the tumors have continued to shrink."

Whew! I breathed a sigh of relief. *That's good news!*

But he didn't *sound* like he was giving me good news. He remained very serious and continued.

"I think we should take a break from chemo to let your body recover."

Yes! Now there was good news!

But still, he remained serious and continued with an explanation of how chemo drugs can cause damage to organs, how there is a limit to how much one person can have in a lifetime. This was all information I had heard before I started treatment.

"Let's take a break for a while and *when* the tumors start to grow again, we will need to start you on another type of chemo—a more aggressive one."

There it was—the dark cloud of hopelessness that had become all too familiar in these appointments.

As we left the doctor's office, I asked my husband, "That was good news, right?" He agreed it was.

"The tumors are shrinking, and I'm done with chemo for a while. That's good, right?"

Then, why did I feel so discouraged?

I spent the next week working through the same old thoughts of hopelessness and feelings of fear and despair. We had reached the end of the line as far as they were concerned. The chemo had worked, but we had gone as far as we could with it, at least for now. There was nothing left to do but wait for things to get worse.

Something in that plan didn't sit right with me. It didn't make sense to sit idly by and wait for things to get worse. God had given me a promise of healing. I knew He had a plan for my life, and I believed He was still working in my situation. I wasn't about to sit around and do nothing while the cancer continued to ransack my body and my life. My doctors had exhausted their expertise, so I did the only thing I knew to do…I prayed.

Then I prayed again.

And I prayed some more.

Through a series of events that I can only attribute to the leading of God, we headed in an entirely different direction. Within the span of a few short weeks, several trusted friends recommended a naturopathic doctor who had success with alternative treatments to cancer.

I had come across some "natural remedies" to cancer in my early research. To be honest, much of it was overwhelming, and some of it was downright odd. At the time, I didn't have the energy or the mental capacity to sift through all of it in addition to all the information being thrown at us by our doctors. Even now, I was rather skeptical of the "alternative route." But we agreed we were desperate and needed to at least hear what he had to say. One week after the appointment with my oncologist, we sat in the naturopath's office.

I told him my story and laid out my medical history. He listened intently and nodded as though he was familiar with situations like mine. He found out we were born-again Christians, and he told us he was also. He asked me questions about my faith, my prayer life, and my belief in healing. Then he looked right at me and said,

"You can beat this. With God's help, you can do this."

Those words struck something deep inside me. We left his office that day with tears of joy, feeling hope for the first time in months.

> *Now faith is the assurance of things hoped for, the conviction of things not seen. (Hebrews 11:1)*

God promised to heal me, and I had assumed that meant miraculously, instantaneously. But God isn't really concerned with our schedules, and He doesn't always work in our timetables.

Just ask Noah.

Faith for the Middle

> *By faith Noah, being warned by God concerning events as yet unseen, in reverent fear constructed an ark for the saving of his household. (Hebrews 11:7)*

Noah took God at His Word and started building an ark. Then he waited. He believed God...and he waited for 120 years to see God's promise fulfilled (Genesis 6:1).

Then there's Abraham and Sarah...

> *By faith Sarah herself received power to conceive, even when she was past the age, since she considered him faithful who had promised. (Hebrews 11:11)*

They believed God and waited...for 25 years before God's promise to them was fulfilled (Genesis 21:5).[2]

And don't forget Joseph...

> *By faith Joseph, at the end of his life, made mention of the exodus of the Israelites... (Hebrews 11:22)*

He received the promise of God in a dream as a young man (Genesis 37:1-11). Then he waited...for 13 years he waited *in a prison* to see God's promise fulfilled.

Of course, there's Moses...

> *By faith Moses, when he was grown up, refused to be called the son of Pharaoh's daughter, choosing rather to be mistreated with the people of God than to enjoy the fleeting pleasures of sin... By faith he left Egypt... (Hebrews 11:24-27)*

He believed God's promise and led the Israelites out of Egypt...then he waited *in the desert* for 40 years!

Are you seeing a pattern? These people took God at His word... *by faith*. God spoke, and they believed. They acted. They chose to "see things that weren't as though they were" simply because God said it would be so.

Because God *always* keeps His Word; it's His nature.

That doesn't mean He does things the way we expect Him to, or the way we would do them. It doesn't mean He adheres to our schedule. But He *always* keeps His promises.

These great heroes of the faith had to wait to see God's promises because there can't be faith without the wait. If God answered our every prayer as soon as we asked, there would be no need for faith. As much as God desires to meet our needs, His greater desire is that we grow in faith.

> *The life of faith is not of mounting up with wings, but a life of walking and not fainting.*
> ~ Oswald Chambers [3]

There's one more thing these stories have in common: They *all* received God's promise because God always keeps His Word!

> *For no matter how many promises God has made, they are "Yes" in Christ. (2 Corinthians 1:20, NIV)*

If you've grown up in church, you're familiar with these stories. You know the beginning *and* the end. If we're not careful, we'll forget about the middle. But that's where life is lived... in the middle.

Yes, Noah heard from God, built a boat, and God saved his family from the flood. But what about the 120 years he spent working on a giant boat when no one had ever seen rain before? He had faith...*in the middle.*

God told Abraham he would have a son and sure enough, Isaac and the nation of Israel were born to a couple well past their prime. But what about the 25 years that he and Sarah spent waiting—month by month—to conceive, knowing that their bodies were incapable of doing so? They had faith...*in the middle.*

Joseph had a dream as a young man, and God sent him to Egypt ahead of his family to save an entire nation from extinction. But what about those 13 years he spent first as a slave, then a servant, then a prisoner? Joseph had faith...*in the middle.*

Moses reluctantly obeyed God and walked an *entire nation* of people across the dry floor of the Red Sea to freedom. But what about those 40 years in the desert when the people grumbled and whined to return to captivity? Moses had faith....*in the middle.*

And what more shall I say? I do not have time to tell about Gideon, Barak, Samson and Jephthah, about David and Samuel and the prophets, who through faith conquered kingdoms, administered justice, and gained what was promised; who shut the mouths of lions, quenched the fury of the flames, and escaped the edge of the sword; whose weakness was turned to strength; and who became powerful in battle and routed foreign armies (Hebrew 11:32-34)

The Bible is full of stories like this...all echoing one glaring theme: God *always* keeps His Word.

You may be in the midst of a storm right now, and you might feel like your world is crumbling around you. But you don't have to fear because you know the One who is unshakable. It doesn't matter what you see with your eyes or what you hear with your ears. It doesn't matter that your situation seems hopeless...that the doctors don't know what to do, that your spouse says it's over, that your employer says you're through, or whatever circumstance is looming big and scary in front of you.

The only thing that matters is that you know the One who holds tomorrow in His hands. The One who calls things that are not as though they were. The One who has promised to never leave you nor forsake you. The One who is...unshakable.

It is by faith you stand firm (2 Corinthians 1:24, NIV)

Becoming Unshakable

It's easy for us to read through the Hall of Faith quickly without realizing the struggle each individual endured *in the middle*. Read Hebrews 11:1-40 again and consider how each example is a testimony of God's faithfulness—a reminder that God *always* keeps His promise.

1. Do you find it difficult to trust God "in the middle" of your situation? Why or why not?

2. How do the stories in Hebrews 11 affect your faith?

3. Which is your favorite story in Hebrews 11? Why?

4. What are you learning "in the middle"?

5. What can you do to strengthen your faith and become unshakable?

Add your story to the "Hall of Faith" in Hebrews 11. In your journal (or in the space below), write "By faith [your name]," and write out your situation. Detail the circumstances stacked against you. Then declare your faith by describing God's promise to you. Write the end of your story (how might God bring you through it) and commit to holding tightly to your faith through "the middle" of your situation.

UNSHAKABLE

UNSHAKABLE CONNECTION
God's Church in Action

Christianity is not a solo sport
~*Larry Osborne*[1]

My husband and I looked knowingly at each other. We had experienced this all-too-familiar moment many times in the last few months.

"Wow," I said.

"Yep," he replied.

"It's like that message was *just* for us."

We'd had this same feeling and similar conversations leaving church almost every week for months, often joking that our pastor should begin his sermons with the following disclaimer: "I'm glad you all came today, but this message is really for Nancy."

For months following my diagnosis, we heard about God's love for us, His compassion for us in the midst of our trials, and His ability to step into those trials and turn them around for our good. Every sermon—every time—applied directly to us and our situation.

Now, as we faced the uncertainty of a new year and a new direction in our treatment plan, our church announced a theme for the year. They've never done that before, and they may never do it again. But they did it then. The theme was simple: VICTORY.

I'm sure they did not have me in mind when they were considering a theme. I am confident my name never came up in the brainstorming meetings. They never said, "I bet Nancy Backues could use some encouragement right now. Let's adopt a theme, just for her."

No, that's not how it happened. But I do believe that God, in a way that only He can, ordered my steps 20 years earlier and led me to a church that would encourage me in my walk and challenge me in my faith. He kept me there when my friends had moved away and chosen other paths. He brought my husband there and called us to raise our family in that community.

At the same time, He was ordering and directing the steps of others: families who would walk with us through this trial, staff members who would come alongside us in the journey, and many others who would encourage us and strengthen our faith. God brought us all together, at the same moment in history, to believe for victory.

I'm not naïve—or arrogant—enough to believe it was all for my sake. If you ask anyone else, I'm sure they would each have a very different story about how, when, and why they came to be in that church at that time.

That's the beauty of how God works. He is able to work *every* detail of your life, my life, and thousands—millions—of other lives together so that at the very moment He wants to reveal something to us, we are in *exactly* the right place at *exactly* the right time.

We can be so sure that every detail in our lives of love for God is worked into something good. God knew what he was doing from the very beginning. He decided from the outset to shape the lives of those who love him along the same lines as the life of his Son. (Romans 8:28-30, The Message).

I had been raised in church; it was not a new concept to me. But as we walked this journey, I came to understand more deeply the impact a local church and its ministry can have on a life and a family.

Often, we went to church emotionally drained and physically exhausted from the toll cancer takes on a family. We were weary, but we went. We went because we needed it.

We needed the worship—not just the lively music and driving rhythm, but the atmosphere alive with adoration of a Savior and expectation of what He would do.

We needed the Word. While we read it daily and consumed it often at home, we needed to be reminded that God is for us and fighting on our behalf. For those darkest days, we needed to come and be refreshed—to find hope to make it through the next week.

We needed the community. Our church is large, but it has always felt like home to us. Still, it had grown even more intimate as people we hardly knew stopped to tell us they were praying for us. I received emails and Facebook messages from people I recognized but had never met. They reached out to let us know they had heard of our need and were praying with us. Many times, we didn't even realize how desperately we needed encouragement. But God knew. And He moved on the hearts of other believers to meet that need.

We needed connection. We all need a support group in life, and that need is stronger when you face a disease like cancer. However, as Christians we need more than a network of well-meaning individuals. We need to be connected to a body of believers.

We spent the greater part of that year hearing sermons on victory and testimonies of victory in the lives of others. Our faith increased, and we believed with expectancy for victory in our own situation.

In June—six months after my last chemo treatment—we found ourselves waiting again for results from the latest PET scan. The doctor went through his usual routine asking how I'd been feeling and examining me for any delayed side effects from the chemo.

Then he quickly reviewed the results: two of the tumors continued to shrink and the third remained stable. With that, he began wrapping up the appointment, and I breathed a sigh of relief, thankful to be free for another few months.

As he reached for the door, he casually mentioned, "If you'd like to talk to a surgeon, I can set that up for you."

I stopped in my tracks.

What? A surgeon?!

Just ten months ago, we had been told surgery would *not* be the goal. I had come to accept the fact that God would intervene or use *other* methods (chemo, alternative treatment) to bring healing.

The doctor continued, "If we can get them out—and I'm not saying we can—but *if* we can, you'll be cancer free…at least for now. It wouldn't hurt to talk to someone."

We agreed we should at least talk to a surgeon. Once again, we left a doctor's office with our minds spinning as we tried to process new information and potentially *another* shift in direction.

Life Is Better Together

After Jesus' crucifixion and resurrection, he left the disciples with one simple instruction: Stay in Jerusalem and wait (Acts 1:4).

They were in crisis. Their lives had been turned upside down. Everything they believed had been destroyed. They had followed Jesus for three years now, living out ministry with him day by day. They believed He had come to overthrow the Roman Empire and usher in a new kingdom on earth. Then they would rule with him.

Instead, the Roman Emperor had crucified Him. Now, Jesus had risen from the dead, confirming that He truly is the Son of God. So *now* He must be ready to establish His kingdom. Nope. No coup in sight. Instead, Jesus took them to a mountaintop, told them to wait, and then left them (Acts 1:6-9).

That must have been one confusing day for the disciples. I doubt they wanted to go back to Jerusalem. They were ready to move on and put it all behind them. But if they had learned one valuable lesson from their time with Jesus, it was this: God always knows best, even when it doesn't make sense to us.

So, the disciples obeyed. They returned to Jerusalem and waited. But they didn't just sit around twiddling their thumbs. They prayed (Acts 1:14).

And God kept his promise; He sent the Holy Spirit. (Read Acts 2:1-13.) He filled the disciples and the believers with power and boldness. He gave Peter a sermon and the courage to stand up and preach. And 3,000 people were saved that day![1]

When we gather together with believers, God shows up and amazing things happen!

> *Where two or three are gathered in my name, there am I among them. (Matthew 18:20)*

This was not a one-night event. The disciples realized if they were going to make it in this world, if they were going to grow in their faith, if they were going to make an impact on a world that had rejected their Savior and now stood against all that they believed, they would need one another.

> *They devoted themselves to the apostles teaching and to the fellowship, to the breaking of bread and to prayer. (Acts. 2:42)*

They *devoted themselves*.... It wasn't simply something they did on Christmas and Easter to keep their grandma happy. It wasn't something they did if there wasn't anything else going on that weekend. It was a priority. Not because they were legalistic and trying to keep up with a list of Christian "do's" and "don'ts." They were committed because they needed to be. They realized "Christianity is not a solo sport." We were meant to do it together.

I realize Christians are not perfect. Nor are all churches filled with warm and fuzzy feelings. I have spent the majority of my life in church—much of that in ministry. I know people have suffered *terrible* wrongs in the name of church and Christianity.

If that is your experience, please hear this: That person who hurt you, or let you down, is simply that: a person...a far-from-perfect, perhaps-entirely-wrong person. Whether it was simply a misunderstanding or a blatant, outright sin, whether they did it intentionally or unintentionally, I'm sorry you were hurt. I'm sorry you were wronged in the name of Christianity. That is not the purpose of the Church. The body of Christ is not meant to injure or maim its members. It is meant to live together in unity.

If one member suffers, all suffer together; if one member is honored, all rejoice together. Now you are the body of Christ and individually members of it.
(1 Corinthians 12:26, 27)

God has designed the Church (capital "C"—the worldwide body of believers in Christ) to bear one another's burdens. That purpose is accomplished practically through the local church (small "c"—a *local* body of believers in Christ). It's through the local church that we connect with the body of Christ (the Church). Church is not just for the hard times, but it's in the hard times that the Church has the opportunity to do what it does best.

If you've been hurt in the name of Church, it can be difficult (even scary) to step out and try to find a place of connection. How do you know where to begin?

Look for a church that...

1. Teaches the Word. There doesn't have to be a memory verse at every gathering, but find a church that teaches the Word of God. You cannot grow in your knowledge and understanding of God's Word if it is not taught.

> *They devoted themselves to the apostles' teaching...*
> *(Acts 2:42a)*

2. Does life together. God has created us with different personalities and interests. Find a group of people with whom you can do life. There's no *style* of church that is more biblical than another. You don't have to like *everything* about a church (chances are you don't like *everything* about your favorite restaurant, sports team, or even your own family!). Find a group with whom you can worship, grow, be challenged, and enjoy life.

> *...to the fellowship, to the breaking of bread...*
> *(Acts 2:42b)*

3. Practices prayer. It's important to find a church that believes in the power of prayer. When you face difficulties (and you will), you will need the strength of their prayers when you cannot pray yourself.

> *...and to prayer (Acts 2:42c).*

Becoming Unshakable

It's easy to think we can do life on our own, until we face something that shakes us and all we believe in. Those are the times we need the support of other believers. But it's often too difficult to find that support then. The disciples understood the need to be connected to other believers, and they committed to doing just that. Read the full story in Acts 2:1-47.

1. Are you committed to a local church? If not, what has kept you from it?

2. What experiences have influenced your view of church?

3. Do you view commitment to a local church as something you "should do" or something you desperately need? Why?

4. How has your local church influenced you in your current circumstances?

5. What would happen if you viewed the local church as a support system, rather than an item on your Christian to-do list? How would it affect which church you attend? How would it affect how often you attend?

Describe your perfect church. What would it be like? How would people dress? How would visitors be welcomed? What would the service look like? Write out a detailed description then reread it. How possible is it for such a church to exist? Could you find one in your area?

UNSHAKABLE VICTORY
God Keeps His Promises

This hope is an anchor for my soul;
my God will stand...UNSHAKABLE
~*Hillsong Church*[1]

After ten months of traditional and alternative treatment, I was suddenly faced with the possibility of surgery once again. To be honest, I wasn't sure I wanted it to be an option. I had come a long way since I sat in the specialist's office ten months earlier and had my hopes of a simple surgery shot down.

I had donned my boots and gone to battle both for my body and my faith. I had endured chemo and was working hard to restore my body and my health. My faith had grown, and I believed God for healing. Surgery seemed like a step in the wrong direction.

To the outside observer surgery probably seemed like the simple fix...get the cancer out, recover, and move on with life. After all, that's what I had thought only a few months earlier. But now, as the person who would be on the table, getting cut open, it didn't seem that clear. Still, there was something alluring about those two glorious words, *Cancer Free*.

Before we headed too far down the road of possibility, we needed to know if surgery was even an option. We agreed to meet with the surgeon, hoping for a simple answer.

Of course, that's not what we got.

He looked at my scans, asked me several questions, and examined my abdomen, back and arm. Then he simply said: "I'm just not sure. It's not really straight-forward."

Of course it's not! Nothing in the last ten months has been!

He wanted to consult with his colleagues then get back to us. Once again we went home without a plan. Once again, all we could do is wait and pray.

A few weeks later, he called to say he had discussed my case with his colleagues, and they agreed surgery would be a *good* option. However, there was still some concern: the tumor in my abdomen could prove to be complicated. It didn't appear to be invading any organs, but they wouldn't know for sure until they "got in there."

Once again we were faced with more questions than answers.

We asked for some time to consider the options, and we continued to pray. I desperately prayed for a clear sign—particularly a large, neon one that read either "Yes, Have the Surgery!" or "No, Do Not Have Surgery!"

I got neither, so we decided we needed more information from people who were smarter than us.

We sent the most recent PET scan to the specialist I had seen 10 months earlier. Since he was the one who originally said surgery would not be an option, I fully expected him to discourage the idea. I was floored when his nurse called and said, "He thinks your case is favorable for removal."

I was so shocked, in fact, I asked her to repeat it. Then I reworded the question a few times, just to make sure I had heard correctly. In ten months we had gone from, "You'll be on some form of chemo the rest of your life; surgery is not the goal," to "Your case is favorable for removal"?

Suddenly, we had all four oncologists on the same page...an experience we had not encountered in almost a year! I scheduled an appointment with my naturopath to get his opinion. I laid out the facts for him and asked him what he thought. He replied, "If they can get it all, I think surgery is a great option!"

Now "5 out of 5 doctors" were recommending surgery. I could not believe it. Still, we did not want to make a decision without knowing we'd heard from God, so we continued to pray.

I pleaded for that big, neon sign.

It never appeared. Instead, we began to see tiny, little signs, and they all seemed to point in one direction: surgery. I wanted to know *for sure*, but the funny thing about faith is...it takes *faith*. Sometimes that means stepping out and trusting God, even when you don't have a big, neon sign.

Once we made the decision and scheduled the surgery, we knew it was the right one. I guess sometimes the neon sign comes *after* we step out in faith.

The fact that God had been with us in every moment of the journey didn't keep me from worrying about the next step. In the days before my surgery, I struggled with the same old emotions—fear and anxiety. My thoughts and emotions were all over the place. The idea of being cancer free in a few short weeks *thrilled* me, and I couldn't help but think of how far God had brought us in only ten months. Still, the thought of another surgery, and all that could possibly go wrong, terrified me.

> *God gave us a spirit **not of fear** but of power and love and self-control. (2 Timothy 1:7)*

If I had learned anything on this journey, it was that fear is not from God. When my thoughts are rooted in fear, anxiety, or worry, it is not God speaking to me; it is the enemy of my soul—the one who seeks to kill me, steal from me, and destroy me. Thankfully, I'd also learned how to handle those fears:

> *We destroy arguments and every lofty opinion raised against the knowledge of God, and take every thought captive to obey Christ. (2 Corinthians 10:5)*

Once again, I waged war on my fear. I battled my anxiety with Scripture: I wrote verses on notecards and read them again and again when I felt afraid. I memorized verses about God's faithfulness and meditated on His promises. Even while my emotions rode a frantic roller coaster, my spirit was at peace in the confidence that God was in control, and He would lead me to victory.

> *We have to choose to be more full of faith than we are of fear.*
>
> ~Chris Caine [2]

I continued to pray for a miracle, hoping the doctor would order another scan and the cancer would be unexplainably gone. That didn't happen.

Thoughts of doubt continued to invade my mind and threaten my peace: Did I need to have more faith? Should I avoid the surgery and stand on faith that God would heal me? Was I allowing doubt and fear to control me by going forward with the surgery?

We had come to trust the expertise of the medical professionals, but even they admitted the outcome was unsure. There simply was no guarantee.

Believing that God had led us every step so far, and trusting that He had given us peace to move forward with the surgery, that's exactly what we did. We never stopped praying for a miracle. I knew God could do it, and I would trust Him for it up to the moment they wheeled me into surgery. Then, I would trust Him to give the surgeon favor, grace, and skill beyond his own expertise.

I don't know why God *didn't* perform a miracle, but I *do* know that God is God, and I am not. He's a lot smarter, a lot wiser, and infinitely more perfect than I am.

*As the heavens are higher than the earth,
so are My ways higher than your ways and My thoughts
than your thoughts. (Isaiah 55:9)*

I also know that when I fix my eyes on God instead of my circumstances, He goes before me and fights for me—every single time. So on August 26, 2014—one year and three days after a diagnosis of "non-curative," metastatic cancer—I went into surgery with great peace, knowing the battle was God's and He would *not* fail me.

> *Fear not, stand firm, and see the salvation of the* LORD, *which he will work for you today…The* LORD *will fight for you, and you have only to be silent. (Exodus 14:13, 14)*

A gifted surgeon skillfully removed a 9-centimeter, malignant tumor from my abdomen without complication. My recovery went well, and we were able to schedule the second surgery six short weeks later. I wrote the word "VICTORY" in giant, red letters in the October 15 space on our kitchen calendar. That was the day the final two tumors were removed in a single surgery.

Fourteen long months after my world was shaken, God led me to victory. It had been a long road, and it wasn't over yet. There would still be weeks of recovery, months of follow-up appointments, years of routine PET scans, and a lifetime of giving my body the nutrition and supplements it needs to stay healthy.

God had been faithful, and I had learned one important lesson: when God promises victory, you can be confident He will deliver on that promise!

> *Thanks be to God, who gives us the victory through our Lord Jesus Christ. (1 Corinthians 15:57)*

Victory in the Air

No one learned that lesson like Joshua.

When God delivered the nation of Israel from Pharaoh, He promised to take them to The Promised Land (Exodus 3:8). Forty years later, only one thing stood between them and their promise: Jericho.

To the Israelites, the fortress city of Jericho must have seemed undefeatable. It spanned eight acres and had walls 30 feet high and 20 feet thick.³ The walls were entirely closed up so that no one went out or came in (Joshua 6:1). There was no easy way for Israel to gain access to—or victory over—the Canaanite city.

The Israelites had endured a long journey from Egypt, including a lengthy detour through the dessert. Babies had been born and loved ones lost along the way. Four decades had passed since they had a place to call home. They were physically and emotionally exhausted. No one would fault them for wanting a break, for asking God to simply step in and do the miraculous. They had seen Him do it before...parting the Red Sea, bringing water from a rock, sending manna from heaven. It wasn't like they didn't *believe* God could do the miraculous. They might have even *expected* Him to do it.

What they didn't know was God planned to do exactly that—the miraculous. He just wasn't going to do it the way they expected.

When Joshua laid out the battle plan, the people must have thought he had gone insane. They were about to attack a fortified city armed with only their voices and a few trumpets? And they were going to give the Canaanites fair warning by marching around the city once a day for six days (Joshua 6:3)? Maybe 40 years in the desert had finally taken its toll on their leader!

The Israelites had a *promise* from God, but Joshua was armed with God's *plan*.

God's promise preceded His plan. *I have delivered Jericho into your hands (6:2).* Before God explained to Joshua *how* He would give them victory over Jericho, He promised him victory was sure. Joshua had God's guarantee that Jericho would fall to the Israelites; it didn't matter how God would bring it about. Joshua simply knew that He would.

UNSHAKABLE

> *Every word of God proves true; he is a shield to those who take refuge in him. (Proverbs 30:5)*

God's plan required faith. *"So Joshua son of Nun called the priests and said to them..." (Joshua 6:6)*. Joshua had to take the promise of God—the promise for victory—back to the people. There was a space of time between the promise and its fulfillment. That space was likely filled with questions— *Was that really God?* (doubt), *Did God really say that?* (fear), *Can we really win this battle?* (worry), *What if God doesn't come through?* (anxiety).

Joshua had to battle his own thoughts and emotions as well as the questions of others. He had to have faith in God's plan because God had already promised the victory.

God's plan required action. *"...the seven priests carrying the seven trumpets before the Lord went forward..." (Joshua 6:8)*. God could have easily stepped in and crushed the walls of Jericho without the Israelites lifting a finger. He had done it before (Exodus 14:13, 14).

But the Israelites had come a long way. They had walked with God for 40 years now, and although they were far from perfect, their faith had increased. They had seen God move on their behalf time and time again. They had seen Him defy the laws of time and space to protect and provide for them. It was time they started using some of that faith that had built up through the desert. God never gives us faith without also giving us an opportunity to use that faith.

God's plan required perseverance. *"They did this for six days" (Joshua 6:14)*. The walls didn't fall the first time the Israelites walked around them. In fact, they didn't even start to shake the first day...or the second or the third. By the sixth day, I'm sure some of the Israelites were beginning to doubt. They might have started feeling a little foolish and even began to wonder if God had forgotten them. But He had not forgotten. His plan was to do far more than give the Israelites a military victory. He was building their faith in the process.

God's plan brought victory. *"When the people gave a loud shout, the wall collapsed" (Joshua 6:20).* I can't wait to find Joshua when I get to heaven. I have so many questions for him about that day: What went through his mind on the sixth time around the city? Was he nervous? Did he doubt? Or was he filled with faith, anticipating what God would do?

In the six days between God's promise and the walls collapsing, I'm sure Joshua faced moments of doubt. I'm sure there were nights when he returned to his tent wondering if he was doing the right thing. There were probably mornings he woke up dreading another lap around the city, longing for the victory to be won already. I know because those are the same emotions I faced, the same struggles I endured while waiting for my victory.

From the beginning, I expected God to intervene and work a miracle in my body. What He did instead was more amazing: He worked a miracle in my life.

At the time of this writing, it's been sixteen months since my last chemo treatment, and I am now *cancer free!* Yes, God healed me, but my healing didn't come as I had expected, or even hoped. Instead of a miraculous intervention that would have rescued me from the storm, God held me tight and took me right through it.

It wasn't what I planned. It's not how I wanted to do it…it's so much better. (God's plan always is!) The lessons I learned through the storm were greater than anything I could have learned without it. God brought me through the storm whole, healed, and stronger than ever.

Whatever you are facing today—or will face tomorrow—you don't need to be shaken.

You don't need to be shaken...because God is good.

You don't need to be shaken...because God really does love you.

You don't need to be shaken...because God is bigger than your circumstances.

You don't need to be shaken...because God has a plan.

You don't need to be shaken...because God's Word is true.

You don't need to be shaken...because the God of Angel Armies goes before you.

You don't need to be shaken...because God is listening and He will answer.

You don't need to be shaken...because God will not send you into battle alone.

You don't need to be shaken...because God will give you victory.

You don't need to be shaken...because God is the One who is UNSHAKABLE.

> *I have set the LORD always before me;*
> *because He is at my right hand,*
> **I shall not be shaken.**
> *(Psalm 16:8)*

Becoming Unshakable

Sometimes our circumstances can seem unbearable, and victory over them can seem unattainable. I'm sure that's how

Joshua felt as he faced Jericho. He did not let his circumstances, or his fears, dictate his outcome. Instead, he chose to take God at His Word and trust Him for victory. Read the full story in Joshua 5:13 to 6:20.

1. What promises from God are you holding onto?

2. In what ways has God promised you victory in your situation?

3. What thoughts or emotions have caused your faith to falter as you believe for victory? How do you combat those thoughts and emotions?

4. What encourages your faith to believe for victory?

5. How has your definition of "unshakable" changed? What does that mean to you now?

Write the perfect ending to your story...the victory as you would like to see it. Then spend some time in prayer, presenting it to God as a request. Consider: Is God leading you to victory in this way? Is there another plan He has? What is He asking you to do *right now* to prepare for the victory He has for you?

Appendix: Becoming Part of God's Family

Recognizing that God loves you and desiring to be part of His family is a great first step, but it is only a step. God's love is a gift, and just as any gift, it must be accepted. Here's how to do that:

1. Admit that you need God. This is the easy part. We all need God. Romans 3:23 says we have *all* sinned. In other words, no one is perfect; we can all agree on that. Romans 6:23 tells us the wages of sin is death. Since we have all sinned, we have all been sentenced to death. And since none of us is perfect, there is nothing we can do to *earn* our way into God's love or His family.

2. Accept Christ as Savior. God graciously offered His only Son, Jesus, to die in our place, therefore paying the penalty for our sin. And, because He also loves us, Christ willingly did so (Romans 5:8, John 3:16). All we have to do is ask Him to forgive us and believe that He does (1 John 1:9).

3. Acknowledge your adoption. When we accept Christ as Savior, we have new life (2 Corinthians 5:17). We are adopted by God and identify with His family. Just as with any adoption, you need to learn about and build relationship with your new family. You do this by reading God's Word, praying, and building relationships with other believers. Commit to reading God's Word on a regular basis and find a Bible-believing community to become part of.

UNSHAKABLE

NOTES

Chapter 1
1 C.S. Lewis, *Mere Christianity* ©1952
2 Holly Wagner, *Warrior Chicks* (Ventura: Regal Press, 2007)

Chapter 2
1 Craig Groeschell, *The Christian Atheist: Believing in God but Living Like He Doesn't Exist* (Grand Rapids: Zondervan, 2011)
2 Max Lucado, *You'll Get Through This* (Nashville: Thomas Nelson, 2013)

Chapter 3
1 Vertical Church Band, "The Rock Won't Move" Band (Provident Label Group, 2013)
2 Mark Batterson, *The Circle Maker: Praying Circles Around Your Biggest Dreams and Greatest Fears* (Grand Rapids: Zondervan, 2011)

Chapter 4
1 F.F. Bosworth, *Christ the Healer* (Grand Rapids: Baker Book House, 1973)
2 Corrie ten Boom, *The Hiding Place* (Grand Rapids: Chosen Books, 1971)

Chapter 5
1 Toby Mac, "Steal My Show" (ForeFront Records, 2012)
2 John Lindell, "The Resurrection and the Life," James River Church, August 25, 2013

Chapter 6
1 Priscilla Shirer, Guest Speaker at James River Church, October 12, 2014
2 Craig Groeschell, *The Christian Atheist: Believing in God but Living Like He Doesn't Exist* (Grand Rapids: Zondervan, 2011)

Chapter 7
1 The City Harmonic, "Praise the Lord" on *Heart* (Integrity Music, 2013)
2 Chris Tomlin, "Whom Shall I Fear [God of Angel Armies]" on *Burning Lights* (sixstepsrecords/Sparrow Records, 2013)
3 Hillsong, "Anchor" on *Glorious Ruins* (Hillsong Church, 2013)

UNSHAKABLE

4 Matt Maher, "Lord I Need You" on *All the People Said Amen* (Provident Label Group, 2013)
5 Hillsong, "Oceans (Where Feet May Fail)" on *Zion* (Hillsong Church, 2013)

Chapter 8
1 Mark Batterson, *The Circle Maker: Praying Circles Around Your Biggest Dreams and Greatest Fears* (Grand Rapids: Zondervan, 2011)
2 Craig Groeschell, *The Christian Atheist: Believing in God but Living Like He Doesn't Exist* (Grand Rapids: Zondervan, 2011)
3 NIV Study Bible (Grand Rapids: Zondervan, 1995), p. 503

Chapter 9
1 Easton's Bible Dictionary, https://www.biblegateway.com/passage/?search=1+samuel+14&versio n=NLT

Chapter 10
1 Newsboys, "We Believe" on *Restart* (Sparrow Records, 2013)
2 Life in the Spirit Study Bible, (Grand Rapids: Zondervan, 1984), p. 40
3 Oswald Chambers, *My Utmost for His Highest* (Grand Rapids: Discovery House Publishers, 1935)

Chapter 11
1 Larry Osborne, "How the Crowd Becomes the Church," James River Church, September 7, 2014

Chapter 12
1 Hillsong, "Anchor" on *Glorious Ruins* (Hillsong Church, 2013)
2 Chris Caine, sermon at *Designed for Life Conference,* October 9, 2014.
3 Life in the Spirit Study Bible, (Grand Rapids: Zondervan, 1984), p. 316
6 Brian Houston, "Ruins Come to Life," James River Church, September 1, 2013

ACKNOWLEDGEMENTS

To all who joined me on my journey and helped make this book possible, a heartfelt thank you…

Wendy Briggs and Kerry Beaman—for the laughter, the tears, and all the chocolate…but most of all for your friendship, support, and invaluable input.

John & Debbie Lindell—for always teaching truth and loving people; you may never know this side of heaven how your ministry has impacted me.

The Best Life Group Ever—your commitment to be "Jesus with skin on" made this journey bearable. We cannot count the times you've gone above and beyond for us.

Grandma Betty—I owe my faith, in great part, to the decades you've spent on your knees for our family. Thank you for every prayer, for every tear, for every act of love.

Rita Backues—for cleaning our bathrooms, doing our laundry, feeding our family and loving our kids; thank you most of all for the amazing man you raised to love me.

Mom and Dad—there simply aren't words to express how grateful I am for all you've done. Thank you for your prayers and for giving of your time and resources. Mom, thank you for cooking, cleaning, and loving my kids. Dad, thank you for teaching me to love God's Word and to stand on its Truth.

Steve—you are the love of my life, and I can't imagine walking through this without you. You have been my rock and my greatest champion. I love you with my whole life.

Abba Father—my "Daddy" God who took me in His arms, held me tightly through the storm, and brought me through to victory. You are an amazing God, my perfect Father.

ABOUT THE AUTHOR

Nancy is an author, speaker, wife, mother, and two-time cancer overcomer. She lives in Missouri with her favorite people—husband, Steve, and children, Olivia and Levi. She writes about faith, family, and embracing grace at www.NancyBackues.com.

CONNECT WITH NANCY ON SOCIAL MEDIA:

WEB: www.NancyBackues.com

FACEBOOK: www.Facebook.com/NancyBackuesWrites

TWITTER: @NancyBackues

PINTEREST: www.Pinterest.com/NancyBackues

UNSHAKABLE

Made in the USA
Lexington, KY
03 July 2015